MARC BOLAN

Wilderness of the Mind

MARC BOLAN
Wilderness of the Mind

JOHN WILLANS/CARON THOMAS

Xanadu

First published 1992 by Xanadu Publications Limited,
19 Cornwall Road, London N4 4PH.

Published simultaneously in trade paperback and in a
limited edition of 1000 numbered copies, casebound in
a slipcase and signed by the authors.

ISBN 1-85480-155-4 (trade paperback edition)
ISBN 1-85480-150-3 (signed, limited edition)

British Library Cataloguing in Publication Data.
A catalogue record for this book is available from
the British Library.

Typeset by The Midlands Book Typesetting Company.

Printed and bound in Great Britain by The Bath Press,
Lower Bristol Road, Bath, Avon BA2 3BL.

FOREWORD

When I was first approached to write something for this book, my immediate reaction was to say no. I felt that the last thing the world needed at this time was yet another Marc Bolan book covering all the same old ground for the purpose of exploiting The Marc Bolan Legend for personal gain.

However, after further discussions with the authors, I realised that these two people were genuine fans (I remembered Caron being at gigs) who were motivated by the sincerest of intentions. They had lovingly spent years collecting and collating material that would have special significance to Marc's admirers, particularly to those who were 'there'.

Marc often joked with me that his doodles, drawings and scribblings would one day be worth millions as I cynically tossed most of them into my waste basket. Of course he may have exaggerated on the value, that was always his style, but he was right, as usual, in that they do have true worth.

One must now be grateful to people like John and Caron who have diligently saved, sought out and finally published their 'treasures' for posterity and the furtherance of Marc's legend. I know Marc would have wholeheartedly approved.

— TONY HOWARD
(Marc's manager, 1972–77)
September 1991

We would like to thank the following people for their help and contributions:

Tony Howard, Morrissey, Mike Pruskin, Tony Prime, Andy Ellison, Mike Mansfield, Hilary Tipping, Roy Carr, Wizard Artists, Westminster Music, Peter Maurice Music, Rex Features, Harry Goodwin, Hamlyn Publishing, Ros Davies, Boz Boorer, Paul Thomas, Gary Smith, Uwe Klee, Nikki Sudden, Mickey Finn, Margaret Nolan, Dave and Marie Rooney, Chris Isherwood, John and Joan Regan, Mary Bullen and, of course, everyone at Xanadu.

This book is dedicated to:

Mark Feld, Mr and Mrs Feld, Harry Feld, Rolan Feld, Gloria Jones, Gavin Ingels, Mike Bezzi, George Rab, Noel Hammond, Martin Barden, Marc Arscott, Karen Hirst, Doreen and Gordon Thomas, Mitchell Thomas, Dennis Gleiwitz, Sara Gleiwitz, Mum and Dad, Graham Willans, Gordon Willans, Rita Willans, Amanda Nicholls, Josi Munns, David Beckett, Vince and Sue, Colm, Steve Gridley, Mark and Tina, Steve Treatment, John and Shan Bramley and Howard Newell.

Mr and Mrs Feld, at their home in Putney, London, 1985.

CONTENTS

MORRISSEY ON MARC

I can't cleverly theorize about Marc; I just loved him, and any judgement of him ultimately sways to a favourable conclusion. But how can it be twenty-one years since I bought my first T.Rex record? After two decades of constant listening I love the songs even more, tho', admittedly, my personal collection thinned out with the advent of Gloria's blanket caterwauling — the voice that signalled the end of the adventure.

Like 'classical' music, pop will endure precisely because of artists like Marc. I cried to certain songs before even knowing the words. My first-ever concert was, obviously, T.Rex at Belle Vue in Manchester in 1972. I spent the night dreaming and watching, permission to fantasize at last. Marc's indeterminate gender (pre-Bowie) excited me because it annoyed so many. The next day I seemed to have a whole new way of thinking about everything, suddenly living in my own personal experience. A Sunday newspaper article was headlined 'Bolan: A Weird Kid With No Friends' and everything was truly clinched. I couldn't actually imagine Notting Hill at all.

A few months later I saw Bowie perform to three hundred people and the big media squabble began. Of course, Marc lost. He lost in the way that pop pioneers always do. The price you pay for being first is that the world as a whole is not always quite ready. When it finally is, you just might be slightly weary, and there's always someone else revving up behind. In the final analysis, Marc and Bowie deserve equal billing, a lifetime away from the Glam-Slade pettiness.

Marc was too intellectual to really make it in America, and I'm glad that he didn't. His lyrical language was truly only graspable in the cosmic imagination, and consequently he is never considered to be a classic British pop writer in the way that, for instance, Ray Davies always is. Interestingly, a Kinks' B-side in 1969 called 'King Kong' has Davies performing a shameless mimic of Marc. Even odder, this B-side was reissued in 1972 as an A-side at a time when 'Rexmania' was at full throttle.

My indispensables are 'Prophets, Seers and Sages', 'My People Were Fair' and 'T.Rex', with 'Metal Guru' as the moment of complete perfection. Marc seemed to age quickly — but under severe public scrutiny, who wouldn't? And, more precisely, who doesn't age anyway?

MORRISSEY

October 1991

· 9 ·

INTRODUCTION

Welcome to *Wilderness of the Mind* — words that originally flowered in Marc Bolan's imagination, as this was the working title for what would have been the follow-up to his book of poetry, *The Warlock of Love*.

This is not yet another Marc Bolan biography, but a book that will take you on a magical trip through segments of Marc's amazing, creative life via a vast amount of previously unseen material — documentation, manuscripts, photographs and interviews.

When we began this project, we did not intend to put together a book that would pander to literary critics; nor were we about to cater to the scandal sheets and gutter press. This book was always going to be for the avid Marc Bolan and T.Rex fan.

Fans ourselves, we thought long and hard about what *we* would like to see in a book about Marc, and came to the conclusion that what was wanted was a collection of as much previously-unobtainable material as possible: unpublished photos, Marc's poetry and stories, his original handwritten notes and so on. Not a journo/writer's 'angle' on Marc's life, but an honest, unadulterated review of that life. Facts, not fiction.

So we have tried to steer clear of writing 'The Marc Bolan Story'; there are enough books already on the market, each with their own interpretation of Marc's life. And with this in mind, we have also omitted a complete discography — although we did feel it appropriate to include a list of Marc's essential albums and singles. After all, it's the music that made us all fans in the first place!

But our main pride in this book comes from the fact that *everything* in it is authentic. We have not tried to elaborate or fabricate any stories, nor have we written anything 'sensational' just for the sake of it. Many of the facts and accounts that have been included were told first-hand to Caron by Marc himself; all the photos and manuscripts are genuine and can be provenanced. Nothing here is exaggerated.

However, you may find details within that contradict your present beliefs. This is, of course, inevitable, when up to now Marc's life has been surrounded by so much guess-work, so many different stories, twisted words and tall tales. (Examples would be, for instance, the blatant fabrications that Marc only ever knew six chords on the guitar and that David Bowie appears on 'The Slider', 'Tanx' and 'Futuristic Dragon' albums, or the rumours that Marc played on 'Nutbush City Limits' (Ike & Tina Turner), 'Ma Ma Ma Belle' (ELO), 'Houses Of The Holy' (Led Zeppelin), David

Bowie's 'Aladdin Sane' album and numerous others . . . No no no!).

Of course, if Marc had been around today, it's possible that he may not have fully approved of the appearance of some things here, as they might be thought to be a little too personal. But being a fan means wanting to know all and everything about Marc. Our problem has been to balance this need with the respect due to Marc's memory when choosing what to include — we, at least, think we have succeeded.

Finally, we hope that you get as much enjoyment from reading this book as we have from writing and compiling it. We feel it is very special, something to be treasured and referred to again and again.

Have fun. And remember — keep a little Marc in your heart!

— JOHN AND CARON

1. FROM HACKNEY TO HEAVEN

We are about to take you on a supersonic joyride through Marc's colourful, musical lifetime. We decided from the beginning to write only a brief biography, for the simple reason that it has been written in full countless times already. So for those of you already familiar with certain parts of the text that is about to follow, we have included unseen photos, manuscripts, handwritten notes etc. along the way, to make your reading that much more interesting and to give you maximum enjoyment throughout.

Remember, Marc's musical history was vast. We are giving you but a fleeting glimpse of the Metal Guru . . .

1947–61

'Marc Bolan' was in fact born 'Mark Feld', on 30th September, 1947 at Hackney Hospital, East London and raised by his parents, Simeon and Phyllis, at the family home, 23 Stoke Newington Common.

From 1952 to 1958, Marc attended Northwold Primary School, before moving to William Wordsworth Secondary in Stoke Newington. It was here that, at the age of eleven, he joined his first pop group. Called Susie & The Hoola Hoops, one of the other members was a friend of Marc's, Helen Shapiro, who would, of course, soon become one of the biggest child stars of the '60s.

In 1961, the whole of Marc's family (including his brother, Harry) upped sticks and moved to Wimbledon, where Marc started to attend Hillcroft School.

1962–64

Marc left school at fifteen and started to try to break into the music scene. He supported himself meantime with various jobs, including serving behind the counter at the famous Two I's coffee bar in Soho, washing up in a Wimpey bar and working at Edgar's Clothing Store (now a branch of the Halifax Building Society) in Tooting, South London.

Marc owned a large number of shirts and suits, and it was this interest in clothes that earned him the title 'King Of The Mods' in the September, 1962 edition of *Town* magazine, where he was photographed by Don McCullin. Around this time Marc was also featured in *Freeman's* catalogue, modelling menswear.

BIOGRAPHY

DECCA GROUP RECORDS

MARC BÖLAN	DECCA

Standin alone in the wood,
With the golden palace bleeding
scarlet tears into the sunset,
I thought of all the treasures -
in the magic palace,
And all the emptiness
in my stomach
and I smiled secretly,
Rememborin the wizard's words.

By the age of seventeen, in order to go with his latest 'folk' image, Marc had decided to call himself 'Toby Tyler'. Under this name, he recorded acoustic versions of Dylan's 'Blowing in The Wind', Dion's 'The Road I'm On (Gloria)' and Betty Everett's 'You're No Good' on acetate formats; but, unfortunately, no record deal came of it.

1965–67

In 1965, Marc met Mike Pruskin. Mike became his manager and had Marc's name changed from Mark Feld to Marc Bolan, before clinching a recording contract with Decca Records, where Marc would record his first single, 'The Wizard'. To promote

Marc Bölan was born in September 1947. After fifteen years had passed he travelled to Paris and met a black magician called The Wizard. He lived for eighteen months in The Wizard's chateau with Achimedes, an owl, and the biggest, whitest Siamese cat you ever saw.

He then felt the need to spend some time alone so made his way to woods, near Rome. For two weeks he strove to find himself and then returned to London, where he began to write.

His writings mirror his experiences with mentionings of the magician's pact with the great god Pan. In London walking down Kings Road, Chelsea in the dead of night he chanced to meet a girl named Lo-og who gave him a magic cat. This cat, named after the girl, is now his constant companion and is a source of inspiration to him.

Now the Wizard's tale is set down for all to hear on Marc's first recording for Decca.

Left and above: items from Decca's 1965 press releases. Note the bogus story of Marc meeting 'The Wizard'. The magic cat Lo-og was Marc's playful reference to the Rolling Stones' manager, Andrew Loog Oldham. Note too the umlaut on the 'o' in Bölan!

the record, Marc appeared on the ITV pop programmes, *Thank Your Lucky Stars* and *Ready Steady Go*; however, neither this single nor the follow-up, 'The Third Degree', would make any dent in the charts. As a result, Marc and Mike mutually agreed to dissolve their management contract in the autumn of 1966.

Later that year, Marc auditioned for the manager-supremo Simon Napier-Bell and under his guidance recorded the track 'Hippy Gumbo', released on the Parlophone label. [Marc also recorded many acoustic tracks that Napier-Bell eventually released on the 1974 LP, 'The Beginning Of Doves'. In 1982 Napier-Bell would use Marc's recordings from the 'Doves' sessions and add various session musicians to produce the album 'You Scare Me To Death', which also included 'I'm Weird', a previously unreleased track written by Marc.] As the single sank without trace, Simon recommended that Marc join John's Children (who he managed at the time), not as lead singer but as lead guitarist and backing vocalist. By the spring of 1967, Marc was not only a fully fledged member of John's Children, but also their major songwriter. One of Marc's compositions, 'Desdemona', was released as their first single on Track Records, but was banned by the BBC because it contained the lyric, 'lift up your skirts and fly'. Marc commented later that the line only referred to a 'witch on a broom'.

Helped by the fact that John's Children appeared on the front cover of the *NME* on 13th May (Marc's first-ever front page), the record received a fair amount of publicity and managed to scrape into the lower end of the charts. However, after a disastrous tour of Germany supporting The Who, Marc decided to leave the band. He had been with them for only three months.

Already by June, 1967, Marc had placed an advert in *Melody Maker* which read:

> 'Freaky lead guitarist, bass guitarist and drummer wanted for Marc Bolan's new group. Also any other astral flyers like with cars, amplification and that which never grows in window boxes.'

Out of this madness came one Steve Peregrine Took, a percussionist and backing vocalist, and Tyrannosaurus Rex was formed. Marc and Steve played a number of gigs and befriended DJ John Peel. The record producer Tony Visconti saw them one night performing at the UFO Club in London and arranged for them to be signed to Regal Zonophone Records.

1968

Tyrannosaurus Rex saw the release of their first single, 'Debora', followed by 'One Inch Rock'. Two albums were also released, 'My People Were Fair ...' and 'Prophets, Seers and Sages ...'. It was during this year that Marc first met Gloria Jones, at a party given by a girl called Marci (of the American band, The GTO's). It would be another five years, however, before she joined T.Rex, at Tony Howard's suggestion.

1969

Marc's book of poetry, entitled *The Warlock of Love*, was published by Lupus on 15th March, and was available through mail order as well as conventional book shops. Marc and Steve released the singles 'Pewter Suitor' and 'King Of The Rumbling Spires' in between which came the album 'Unicorn'. After the release of the LP, Tyrannosaurus Rex toured the States; but by the end of the tour Steve Took had made the decision to quit. Marc, on his return to England, advertised once again through *Melody Maker* for a replacement. This time the advert read:

> 'Tyrannosaurus Rex — wanted to work with T.Rex, a gentle young guy who can play percussion, i.e. bongos and drum kit, some bass guitar and vocal harmony, photos please.'

Marc eventually recruited Mickey Finn into a partnership that was to last until 1975. Mickey was the only member of T.Rex other than Marc to receive a percentage of royalties; the other members of the band, recruited later, would be waged.

1970

On 30th January, Marc married his girlfriend and *confidante*, June Child, at the Kensington Registry Office, on what appeared to be a mere whim; as he said, 'it seemed like a funky thing to do at the time'.

In September, Marc had made the decision to abbreviate the name Tyrannosaurus Rex (a DJ's nightmare) to the more pronounceable T.Rex. At the same time, Regal Zonophone, Marc's record label, announced that they too would be having a name change, and in future would be known as Fly Records. The single 'By The Light Of A Magical Moon' and the album 'A Beard of Stars' were both released before the

Above and right: Marc relaxing at home—57 Blenheim Crescent, Notting Hill, London W11—in 1970.

changeover, however; the first Fly single, 'Ride A White Swan', was also T.Rex's first *big* hit, stumbling its way to the No. 2 slot, while the album 'T.Rex' also did well.

1971

It was not until the release of 'Hot Love' in February of this year that the media really began to take notice of the strange, elfin-like creature that was Marc Bolan. Kids bought the single in their droves, giving T.Rex their first No. 1 smash hit. The success of 'Hot Love' also helped push the 'T.Rex' LP as high as No. 12 in the charts and in turn forced Fly Records to issue a 'Best Of' compilation. This contained the bonus of previously unreleased 'A Beard Of Stars' outtakes, 'Once Upon The Seas of Abyssinia' and 'Blessed Wild Apple Girl'.

With the release of 'Get It On', a song partly inspired by Chuck Berry's 'Little Queenie', Marc had his second No. 1, proving to the doubting Thomases that T.Rex were more than just a one-hit wonder. 'Get It On' remains a timeless piece of classic pop, carved in the wizardry of the three-chord trick.

T.Rex were now hot property; even the tabloid press were clamouring for an interview or photo. Marc was always happy to oblige. Stories of his time spent with the 'wizard' he met in France, how his latest projects with Ringo or Bowie were getting along, even what was thrown into his dustbin that morning: it was all headline news.

The year also brought them their first truly classic No. 1 LP, 'Electric Warrior', a record that should be considered an all-time great; with it, Bolan really made his mark on the rock and pop world, finally hitting on a formula and style that would leave music-lovers gasping for more. This album was also the first to include Marc's new recruits: Steve Currie (bass) and Bill Legend (drums).

Now the hits were coming like wildfire, but even Marc's 'Jeepster' could not budge Benny Hill's 'Ernie (The Fastest Milkman In The West)' from the No. 1 spot. There was obviously a large section of the British public that were, shall we say, *confused* at this time. However, T.Rextasy had begun.

1972

On 21st January, a taster for the forthcoming album ('The Slider') was released on

Right: Chelita Secunda's letterhead, 1972. Directors M. and J. Feld are of course Marc and June. Chelita was married to Tony Secunda (Marc's manager at the time), who introduced her to Marc and suggested that she become his personal assistant.

CHELITA SECUNDA.

WARRIOR MUSIC PROJECTS LIMITED
16 DOUGHTY STREET LONDON WC IN 2PL
01 242 3110 · 01 405 2995

MERCHANDISING, PR and PERSONAL ASSISTANT TO MARC BOLAN and T-REX

 DIRECTORS :———— M FELD J FELD K F LINGE P D CARROLL

Marc's own Wax Co. label. This was 'Telegram Sam', which had advance orders of over three hundred thousand. In no time at all 'Telegram Sam' has rocketed its way to No. 1 and the song, inspired by a messenger Marc had once had in the States, was adding to what was to become a golden trail of hits.

'The Slider' LP was eventually released in the summer of 1972. It remains an album rich in lyrical content and wordplay, and was an exceptional follow-up to 'Electric Warrior'.

Mass hysteria was, of course, the order of the day and with 'Metal Guru' and 'Children Of The Revolution' scooping up the pocket money of thousands of teenagers all over the British Isles, it was announced that T.Rex were now the biggest-selling act since The Beatles.

Adding yet another string to his bow, Marc collaborated with none other than ex-Beatle Ringo Starr, to make the ever-so-slightly-surreal feature film, *Born To Boogie*. Consisting of a collage of cuts of, variously, T.Rex's two sell-out concerts in March at the Empire Pool, Wembley, Marc himself, a jamming session with Elton John and Ringo Starr playing 'Tutti Frutti' and 'Children Of The Revolution', a mad hatter's tea party and so on, it was slated by some contemporary critics. But it remains Marc's epitaph, in that it was the only professional concert footage to be filmed and released in his hey-day, an absolute must for anyone wishing to know why Marc and T.Rex were *the* band of the time.

A new single followed, 'Solid Gold Easy Action', in which Marc tipped his hat to Mick Jagger, with the line 'I can't get no satisfaction'. While in the States, Mick had apparently given Marc some coaching in live performance technique (if anything rubbed off, it remains invisible to us). The song was, of course, a smash and paved the way for another grand appearance on *Top Of The Pops*. This, along with 'Metal Guru' and 'Children Of The Revolution', is one of Marc's three finest performances available on video; these are definitely worth a look (available on 'The Ultimate Video Collection' [Telstar, 1991]).

As Christmas approached, a flexi-disc was sent out to all T.Rex fan club members as a special present from Marc and the band.

1973

As tends to happen with all major stars, the press started a backlash against Marc, with accusations that his singles had become a family of clones. His answer? The release of two staggering rock singles which, quite simply, blew the competition away.

The first of these two releases was '20th Century Boy'. This, with its layers of guitar and heart-stabbing riff, finally showed the critics what Mr Bolan was made of; although the song has been covered numerous times since then, by bands such as REM, Girlschool and Siouxsie & The Banshees, none of these versions hold a candle to the original.

Secondly came 'The Groover'. As with so many of Marc's compositions, the lyrics had sexual overtones to them, this time with a rhythm track to match. However, Marc was always clever enough not to make his meaning so blatant that the BBC would be forced to impose a ban.

In between these two came the album 'Tanx' which, as the word play in the title suggests, was a kind of thankyou to everyone that had bought records in the past. An unusual album that did not contain any singles (except for 'Born To Boogie', which was a B-side), it remains many's favourite, as it captures a strange, atmospheric quality. A lovely album in a space and time of its own. (One of the tracks on the album, 'Left Hand Luke', was originally written for Aretha Franklin, although we doubt if she's ever heard it!)

On 10th August, Marc, along with Gloria Jones, Pat Hall and Stephanie Spruill, released a semi-instrumental track entitled 'Blackjack'. As he did not want this to be considered a T.Rex track, Marc did not release it on the usual Wax Co. label, but had it issued on the standard EMI label instead. This was probably just as well, as the single sunk without trace; however, like many flops made by major artists, it has now become yet another collectable item.

To close 1973, Marc released 'Truck On (Tyke)' as a single. Not too much can be said about this, as it is not representative of Marc at his best: despite great verses, the chorus sounds as if it was simply made up on the spot, without any prior thought.

By this time, T.Rex had sold over forty-seven *million* records worldwide, and were dominating both the press and the charts. Their year of success was marred only by the departure of drummer Bill Legend (who was replaced by an ex-member of the 60's band Eire Apparent, Davey Lutton) and, after three years of marriage, the break-up of Marc and June.

1974

The year began with the release of what is best described as a book of words put to music. 'Teenage Dream' was a blockbuster of Bolanic poetry, but undoubtedly the wrong choice for a single. If you listen to the LP 'Zinc Alloy' you will see what we mean: if Marc had released the album opener, 'Venus Loon', it would surely have put him back on top with its immortal lines, 'First girl I ever loved I don't recognise; her nose is smashed, her frame is bent, she's covered in flies'. What more could you ask? Sadly, this was the last album to use the production talents of Tony Visconti.

It was also around this time that keyboard player Peter Leslie (Dino) Dines (ex-Keef Hartley) joined the ranks of T.Rex.

Mid-1974 saw Marc's weight grow to Elvis-like proportions, fuelled by drugs and brandy. However, to promote the release of 'Light Of Love', Marc starred in a video: although the song was quite ordinary, this psychedelic style promo was utterly brilliant and all was forgiven. Until, that is . . . the final single of the year. 'Zip Gun Boogie' was a bland recording, built around stale, repetitive lyrics, which stemmed from an earlier 'gospel' song written by Marc. (This was tentatively called 'Sky Church Music' and a demo version of it can be found on the 'Rarities Three' album issued by the Marc Bolan fan club.)

Marc's relationship with singer/songwriter Gloria Jones blossomed throughout the year; in December it was announced that she was pregnant with Marc's child.

1975

This year's album release, 'Bolan's Zip Gun', was the most disappointing LP to date, a mish-mash of over-produced and lyrically over-zealous songs. However, every T.Rex album still has its golden moments, the most precious here being the track "Till Dawn" (a song that remains one of Marc's most beautiful ballads), with the mid-tempo 'Precious Star' rating as a possible silver moment. This was also the last album to feature Mickey Finn.

Then, what had started off as a bad year suddenly turned around with the release of a strange little song, about a frog, called 'New York City'. Whether it rose up the charts on novelty value or not, it took Marc right back into the Top Twenty.

The follow-up, 'Dreamy Lady' also headed in the right direction. For anyone who thinks that Marc was not ahead of his time, we suggest that they search out the punk/glam performance he gave to promote this single on ITV's *Supersonic* (available on the video called '20th Century Boy').

Marc and Rolan, September/October 1975.

Above: Marc leaving the T. Rex office in New Bond Street, July 1975.

Right: Photo of Marc, Gloria and Rolan, signed by Marc and Gloria, January, 1976.

And finally, on 26th September, the same day that 'Dreamy Lady' was released, Gloria gave birth to Marc's son, Rolan Seymour Feld (or Rolan Bolan).

1976

In February, T.Rex began to tour extensively around the UK in order to promote the new album, 'Futuristic Dragon', a tour which contained the most dates they had played in Britain since the 'Electric Warrior' gigs of 1971.

Marc recorded various alternative versions of songs featured on the 'Futuristic Dragon' album, such as 'All Alone', 'Sensation Boulevard', 'Dawn Storm', 'New York City', 'Dreamy Lady' and 'Chrome Sitar', some of which are arguably even better than the final cuts and which will, hopefully, become available one day. Nevertheless, the end product still shines, remaining one of the most underrated T.Rex albums to date.

The first single release of the year was 'London Boys', a disappointing, weakly-produced record that failed to reach the Top Forty and that was felt to be inappropriate for inclusion in the 'Dragon' album.

However, on 5th June, Marc released a song entitled 'I Love To Boogie', a two minute slice of genius that was a cross between the old T.Rex style and rock-a-billy, inspired by Webb Pierce's 'Teenage Boogie'.

Shortly after the release of 'Boogie', Tony Howard recruited Miller Anderson. Originally Anderson was supposed to be *lead* guitarist, in order to solve the problem of Marc's rather limited soloing ability; Marc did not like this at all, but as he did agree with Tony that Anderson would be an asset to the band, he eventually joined T.Rex as rhythm guitarist/backing vocalist.

Singing 'Boogie' and the follow up, 'Laser Love' (the last record to feature drummer Davey Lutton and long-time bassist Steve Currie, who would demand and receive a payoff of the grand sum of one hundred pounds), Marc appeared headlining a show from Wimbledon called *Rollin' Bolan*, which, when shown, featured five of his songs and made it seem as if Marc could finally be on the way back . . .

In July, June Feld/Bolan, filed for divorce, citing Gloria Jones as co-respondent. A decree-absolute was never obtained, however.

1977

Marc and Gloria kicked off the new year with a cover version of Phil Spector's old Teddy Bears' classic, 'To Know Him Is To Love Him'. In itself, this was a fair attempt, but it was overshadowed by the amazing B-side, 'City Port', which hypnotises the listener with the strange Bolanic tune and the quite stupendously cryptic lyrics. This was the only record, other than the Big Carrot single of 1973, to be issued on the plain EMI label in Marc's lifetime.

On 11th March, Marc's new album, 'Dandy In The Underworld', was released. Marc was extremely proud of this album, releasing two tracks as singles: 'The Soul Of My Suit' and the title track, 'Dandy In The Underworld'.

Seeing the latest trend of punk rock as a breath of fresh air, Marc booked The Damned as support act on the 'Dandy' tour; then, with his new T.Rex (Tony

Right: **Photo of Marc and girlfriend Gloria Jones with The Shadows at the Royal Garden Hotel, Kensington, West London, in May 1977.**

Newman [drums], Herbie Flowers [bass], Dino Dines [keyboards] and Miller Anderson [guitar]), suddenly found that he was playing to ecstatic audiences throughout Great Britain and once more receiving press acclaim. Gone was the podgy, drug-addicted has-been of 1975: here was the Bolan everyone had wanted back, a twenty-nine year old punk on the verge of a glorious renaissance.

Quick to cash in on Marc's new-found success, Cube Records released the EP 'Bolan's Best + One' on 5th August, which included an unreleased track from 1969 called 'Demon Queen'. In an interview Marc stated that, 'It's not a real record. It sounds like I've got no hands. It's a bit of a con, really.'

Not content with a successful album and tour under his belt, Marc then negotiated and made his own six-part television series for Granada TV called, simply, *Marc*.

Then, on 16th September 1977, on their way home from Morton's Restaurant, Berkeley Square, Gloria crashed their Mini into a tree in Barnes, killing Marc and injuring herself badly. Marc's mother has told us that he was found in the back seat of the Mini (thrown there, presumably, by the force of the impact) and that the only mark on him was a slight scratch on his face. Marc had often said in interviews that he would not live to see his thirtieth birthday; he would have been thirty just two weeks after he died.

Marc had released just one more single before his death, called 'Celebrate Summer'; since then there have been many reissues and compilations of Marc's material. But, as with Jimi Hendrix, Jim Morrison, Janis Joplin and Elvis Presley, no one likes to hear their idol's music tampered with. Worst of all, we think, are the remixes and 'new' albums that have been doctored and edited by various producers and session musicians, none of whom seem to understand anything about Marc's very special sound, feel and creativity. No matter what the intention, the real fans will always prefer to hear a track 'unfinished', rather than glossed over with the work of unknown quantities.

Left: Posing outside the T. Rex office at 69 New Bond Street, London W1, on 13th September, 1977. The arm on the left belongs to Marsha Myers, Marc's personal secretary at this time. The photo was taken just three days before Marc's death.

2. TALKIN' ABOUT THE 'FLEETFOOT VOODOO MAN'

None of the interviews in this chapter have ever been published before; and, with the exception of the Mickey Finn interview, all of them were conducted by the authors. They are presented here with a minimum of editorial exaggeration or fabrication, transcribed verbatim from tapes.

The Mike Pruskin Interview was conducted in the living-room of his Kensington home on 26th February, 1991. Mike, a very polite man who offered us Earl Grey tea and food as we began talking about Marc, was slightly hesitant at first, but became more relaxed as he realised that we were not journalists out for a sensationalised story, but genuine fans. He is now married with one son, and is the owner of a successful Art Deco gallery/business in the heart of Kensington.

The Andy Ellison Interview took place in the upstairs living-room of his beautifully-furnished Hampstead home on 15th October, 1991. We began talking about Marc while being supplied with cups of coffee by Andy's wife (who looked a little like Sandie Shaw). Andy himself was enthusiastic and genuine while talking about Marc, and he came across as very warm and friendly.

In the '60s, Andy was lead singer with the psychedelic group John's Children, and worked with Marc for a time. He later went on to form Jet in 1974 with ex-John's Children drummer, Chris Townson. Then, in 1977 he formed his own band, Radio Stars, who had a Top 40 hit with 'Nervous Wreck'. The single's B-side contained a Bolan composition called 'Horrible Breath'.

Andy now owns two houses, one in Hampstead and one in Brighton. He works *ad hoc* painting and decorating, while still keeping his hand in recording and writing. He is happily married with two daughters.

The Mickey Finn Interview: Mickey was Marc's percussionist from 1969 to 1975. According to Micky Marmalade, Mickey Finn was taken off various tracks during the 1974–5 period due to his drug problems, which were affecting his playing and timing; without his knowledge, he was replaced by an American female percussionist called Bobbye Hall Porter. While on tour in the US in 1974, Alphi O'Leary (Marc's chauffeur/bodyguard) found Mickey drugged up in bed when he should have been ready to catch a flight to the next gig. After several unsuccessful attempts to persuade him to get out of bed, Alphi was finally forced to pick Mickey up and throw him into a bathful of cold water.

Even after this, Mickey managed to miss the flight and had to catch a later plane. He eventually turned up, just in time for the gig, but too late for a sound check. Marc was furious at Mickey's unprofessional behaviour and would not speak to him or acknowledge his presence either during or after the show.

In fact, contrary to popular belief, Mickey did not leave the band to pursue a solo career: he was sacked by Marc. Mick O'Halloran, Marc's personal roadie, says that while Marc was planning a Stateside visit he called their manager, Tony Howard, and instructed him to tell Mickey that 'his services [were] no longer required'. This must have been a devastating blow to someone who had not only been a faithful member of the band, but a close friend of Marc's over the years.

The interview reproduced here was conducted over the telephone by an American journalist in 1974; the tape from which it was copied has only recently come to light. Mickey himself is still involved in music, and currently lives in South Norwood, London.

The Mike Mansfield Interview was conducted on 12th September, 1991, in Mike's own studio off Carnaby Street, while the legendary TV producer of *Supersonic* fame and his assistant, Hilary Tipping, took a break from working on his latest show, *Cue The Music*.

Right: Marc with Mike Pruskin, 23rd October, 1965.

THE MIKE PRUSKIN INTERVIEW

Mike Pruskin was Marc's manager from 1965–6. These are his recollections of him twenty-five years on . . .

'I first met Marc while I was working as a freelance publicist for The Nashville Teens and Them. Marc came into my office in Wardour Street. He was very ambitious and had lots of ideas. I thought he had something — he definitely had a strong charismatic quality. Anyway, the company I was working for didn't think the same way as I did — they were a bunch of creeps — so I left and decided to work with Marc.

'We had a contract drawn up between us, and decided that we should get a place together, so we moved into a basement flat at 22 Manchester Street, London W1. The rent was eight pounds a week. For that, we had a living-room, kitchen, two bedrooms, and also a telephone — a luxury in those days.

'At this time we were trying to find a more catchy name for Marc, and came across a French fashion designer called Marc Bohan. We originally thought his name was Marc Boham, so we changed it around a little and put an umlaut on top of the 'o' of Bolan, and Mark became 'Marc'. There was no special reason for this, we just thought it was kind of interesting. It was Marc and I who decided on the name before Decca got involved — even the early acetates had 'Marc Bölan' on the labels. We decided on that, no-one else, contrary to other stories that I've heard.

'Marc was writing a lot at this time — stories, poems, songs, anything really, although there weren't many songs you could call finished, as he used to chop and change from one thing to another. The only real, completed songs were 'The Wizard' (originally entitled 'The Wizard In The Woods') and 'The Third Degree'. I remember Marc writing these songs in our flat, and also another song called 'Rings Of Fortune', which later appeared on 'The Beginning Of Doves' album.

'With just these few songs in hand we went to see someone called Leslie Conn who had an agency in Denmark Street. He introduced us to Jim Economides and helped us get the Decca contract. The trouble was, Jim was so straight, he wanted to make Marc sound American West Coast, and lined up songs by Burt Bacarach and Hal David for Marc, although he never recorded any of those songs.

'In the summer of 1965 we went into Decca's studios in Broadhurst Gardens, West Hampstead and Marc recorded 'The Wizard' and 'The Third Degree'. All the people involved were session musicians. The Ladybirds were the backing vocalists and Mike Leander, who later worked with Gary Glitter, did the arrangements (he was in fact regularly employed by Decca at the time). As I recall, Marc didn't play guitar on 'The Wizard', but he did play some guitar on 'The Third Degree'. Looking back on it, 'The Wizard' was very naïve, and although this was Marc's first big break, he was very nervous at the time. I thought the arrangement on 'The Wizard' was too straight; the B side, 'Beyond The Rising Sun', was much better. Marc was very good with his vocal; it didn't take him very long to record it at all. In fact, the whole session only took half a day to complete. Marc didn't have *that* voice then (the strong vibrato). He used to try and sound more like a cross between Bob Dylan and Cliff Richard. Although he was practising a great deal with his guitar, Marc still thought that he was going to be a slick American filmstar, like James Dean. You see, we lived across the road from Ken Pitt (David Bowie's manager in the early days), and Ken used to be involved with Bob Dylan and, believe it or not, James Dean. Marc's dream was to

Marc outside his flat in Manchester Street, 23rd October, 1965.

be like James Dean, he wanted to die young and be just like him. Marc definitely didn't want to grow old.

'Around this time we obtained a publishing deal, though a very poor one. We got fifteen pounds a time for one thing we did, and then sixpence for something else. We didn't make any money out of it, but at least we were heading in the right direction.

'He did have some other guy involved with him, called Les Thomas, who tried to arrange gigs and things, but he did nothing for Marc — he was too wishy-washy. In fact, Les Thomas used to be involved with David Jones (who later became David Bowie). Bowie had been around a long time too — he had no money either. I remember lending him a pound once, he was desperate for money. He never paid me back, mind you! Marc and I used to see David hanging around. They weren't great friends at the time, though they sometimes used to go for a drink together at the Giaconda Coffee Bar in Denmark Street.

'Marc was always very aware of clothes and fashion. He wore these suede mosquito boots that he used to buy from Milletts in Charing Cross Road. Even the way he picked them was very precise — they had to be a certain colour and style. He only had a 24″ waist at the time, he was a very tiny person. He often wore these thin corduroy trousers, which of course had to fit perfectly! Later on, we did a wonderful deal with Jon Michael, the designer. We got some amazing leather coats and shirts in exchange for giving him some publicity.

'Marc's major musical influence at this time was Bob Dylan. He would take a phrase from a Dylan song and expand it. He was very much into Dylan's first album, and 'The Times They Are A Changing'. He also listened to Dylan's 'Blonde On Blonde' album a lot, and really wanted to get more serious about playing the electric guitar. Funnily enough, I don't ever recall Marc looking at any chord books, it's a miracle how he ever learned to play in the first place.

'I remember he used to hate Donovan. He always said to me that he thought Donovan was a kind of 'diluted' Dylan. Marc also wasn't keen that Donovan wore similar clothes to himself — the mosquito boots and the like.

'Marc also loved the blues, and in particular, Bessie Smith, though I'm sure that was just because George Melly (who we got very friendly with) was into Bessie Smith himself! We saw a lot of George Melly, who used to work for *The Observer*. George was attracted to Marc, and through him we ended up getting an article in the paper.

'We were pushing ourselves in every direction to get all the publicity we could. We had some lovely photographs taken at Highgate Cemetery in the snow, amongst the statues and crypts. A photographer I knew, called Tony Prime, took them. He took a lot of photos of Marc around that time — he also worked for *The Observer*.

'We did a wonderful interview with *Queen* magazine (now *Harpers & Queen*). This was one of the first interviews where Marc told the story of the black magician in Paris. However, the interviewer got hold of the wrong end of the stick and thought that Marc meant that the magician was coloured; in the interview she stated that Marc lived with a "coloured magician" in Paris! It was a good story, but all a load of hype — you know that, don't you? Marc would do anything to get publicity in those days, and whatever coverage we'd get, we'd get together. We were constantly hustling for

Above and following pages: Marc photographed by Tony Prime in Highgate Cemetery, 1965.

promotion. That's not to say we didn't make any mistakes. We did a terrible interview for *The Evening Standard* in 1965 [published 23rd October, 1965]. The interviewer, Maureen Cleave, just edited in anything she wanted to say. Marc and I hated it — I think we hid for a week! Don't forget, we were both very young. We were coming out with statements like "Marc will be bigger than Elvis" — awful!

'We managed to get on *Ready Steady Go* [transmitted on ITV networks, December, 1965. Marc performed 'The Wizard' — not available on video] as we were very friendly with Vicky Wickham, who was producing the show at that time. We also did *Thank Your Lucky Stars* in Birmingham [sang 'The Wizard'; also transmitted on ITV networks sometime in 1965. Video not available]. We had to catch a taxi all the way there as it was filmed on a Sunday, and in the 60's there were no trains or coaches on Sundays! The taxi cost us about twenty pounds. I don't know how we made any money. We received hardly any royalties for 'The Wizard'. We did get paid something like thirty pounds for appearing on *Ready Steady Go*, but even though we had a contract together, we just split the money fifty-fifty.

'After the *Ready Steady Go* appearance, a Marc Bolan fan club was formed by a girl in Teddington, Middlesex. Marc and I went to visit her and spent the whole day there. I can't remember her name, she was only very young, about fifteen/sixteen. We used to supply her with photos and newsletters to send out, although there weren't too many members! However, it was 'The Wizard' that gave her the incentive to write to Decca in the first place.

'Marc only ever did two gigs while I was with him. The first was at a little place in Richmond, Surrey, called "The Pontiac". The second one was in Wembley, a student gig, it was one of those ten-bands-on-the-bill events. Marc used an electric guitar and amplifier that I bought for him at this gig, but it was a total disaster because the amp didn't work very well so we ended up getting a replacement from The Nashville Teens, who were also on the bill. The whole thing went bankrupt, no-one got paid. Even though Marc wasn't very good at playing the guitar, it was in his favour that he was very good-looking and had an amazing personality, though very naïve. He was though, very good at chords. He had good phrasing, even though he used a different sort of voice to that he used later on. At both gigs he used the Cliff Richard/Bob Dylan voice that he had at the time. Marc never wanted to get a band together, he always wanted to do it on his own. I don't think he was confident enough to become a fully-fledged musician, and later on he even flogged the electric guitar and amp that I bought him because we needed the money.

Marc on stage, playing semi-electric guitar at a one-off student gig at Wembley, 1965.

'Marc wasn't very sociable, he wouldn't go out a lot, only to do work. He didn't like going to clubs or anything; we used to go to three or four parties a night, sometimes, for business reasons, but Marc would always stay at home if he could. Sometimes we used to go to the Marquee in Wardour Street. I remember we used to cadge lifts off people so we wouldn't have to walk home. Rod Stewart was playing there once with Steampacket, and after the gig we all piled into their jeep and got a lift home. It was like that in those days, very friendly — we knew people like Eric Clapton, Jeff Beck and Brian Jones.

'I never knew if Marc was straight or gay because he used to play a lot of games with everyone, he was everything to everybody. Marc's girlfriend at the time was called Terry. I knew her very well, as she used to stay a lot in our Manchester Street flat. She looked just like a boy and I remember they used to wear each other's clothes. Terry was very sweet and totally in love with Marc, she would do anything for him.

'Although Marc was very charming to be with, it got very tiring towards the end trying to arrange things for him, and we were fed up of never having any money, so we decided to go our separate ways. We left our flat, without paying the rent. I went to America for two years, and Marc got quite friendly with Jim Economides at Decca. Although Jim didn't become Marc's manager in the true sense, he did try to develop Marc as an artiste. However, this relationship was short-lived, as Jim also left for the States, and that's when Marc got involved with Simon Napier-Bell.

'I did follow Marc's career vaguely. I think he got a lot better. 'The Wizard' was too derivative at the time — don't forget he was *very* young, but he grew and became very good. I never saw Marc again, I should have but I never did. I felt that what's past is past, and to get to see him would have been difficult anyway. I have very fond memories of our time together, though. He was an extremely interesting person to have known ...'

THE ANDY ELLISON INTERVIEW

'The first time I actually met Marc was when my manager, Simon Napier-Bell, drove me to where Marc's parents lived, a pre-fab in Wimbledon just around the corner from the dog track.

'Simon introduced me to Marc before leaving, then Marc's Mum and Dad went out and left us to it. Marc went into the kitchen and cooked us both some mushrooms on toast, before showing me a weird and wonderful book that he was reading, called *The Tin Drum*. After our mini-banquet, we sat together and began to write some songs in his bedroom. It was at this first session that he actually began writing 'A Midsummer Night's Scene'. Marc had a lot of songs already written, things like 'Cat Black' and 'Desdemona'.

'I didn't make the decision to have Marc in the band. It was Simon. He just said, "Go around and have a go, see what happens. If it works, fine." I was, in fact, the guinea-pig — I had to see if we could work together, then report back to the other members of John's Children.

'Contrary to what people think, we did, believe it or not, work very hard in the studio. It only turned into chaos when we got on stage. I remember when 'Desdemona' was banned. We all had a laugh about it and thought it might even enhance sales. We thought that being banned was quite an exciting thing to happen.

'It's strange to think back now, but Marc was never perturbed about not being able to sing lead vocal. He seemed to be quite happy, at that stage, to play guitar while I sang. Anyhow, it was down to Simon where Marc's vocals went on the records. Marc didn't really have a say in it. Simon was producing, so he told Marc what to do and where to sing. I remember recording 'A Midsummer Night's Scene' and Simon mixing it again and again. There must have been something that he felt wasn't quite right. Whether or not Marc had said something to him I don't know, but the rest of the band didn't. There must have been at least a dozen different mixes of that song — they're floating about somewhere.

'We performed lots of songs that Marc wrote, but for some reason we never recorded them: things like 'Cat Black', 'Jasper C. Debussy' and 'Menthol Dan'. There may be very rough demos around but not that I can remember. I can recall 'Sally Was An Angel' — both Marc and myself sang lead vocals on it. I would sing one verse, Marc would sing the next and so on. That's definitely on tape somewhere.

'I never thought Marc's lyrics were too "airy-fairy"; they were just off the wall and slightly mad, which was why I liked them! I don't think the words meant anything; they just conjured up pictures, more than anything else.

'I always found Marc to be a very private person, although he could switch from one role to another. One minute he would be nice and sweet and the next he could be deadly vicious. But that said, he was still much quieter than the rest of us, especially off stage. While we'd all be going crazy, like leaping out of the cars on autobahns [the motorways in Germany] and smashing things up, he'd sit quietly in the car and write poetry and things. He was constantly writing. We used to say to him, "Will you *stop* writing that stuff, Marc?" and grab the piece of paper off him — and sometimes he'd break down in tears! On stage however, he was *very* forceful. When we toured Germany with The Who there were riots — we were absolutely crazy and Marc was just as violent as the rest of us. He was heavily into it. He brought these chains along with which he used to smash the stage, his guitar and his amplifier, and he'd roll about on the floor, or balance his S.G. on his head. He bought his S.G. Gibson off Trevor White [from The A-Jaes].

'The Who tour we did in Germany was something else. They didn't like us one bit, from the night that we arrived. We had these Jordan amplifiers shipped over from America, which were the most powerful amps in the world at the time, and we used to join them all together to produce this wall of sound that was much better than The Who's Marshall complex. When we began our soundcheck at Nuremburg, it was so loud that Townshend and Daltrey came out on stage, because they thought we were using their equipment — they all stood around amazed. From that moment on there was this kind of jealousy. Eventually, they asked if they could borrow our stuff one night because, they said, their equipment was mucked up. Anyway, we let them. It was, however, just an excuse to smash it all up on stage. I remember Pete Townshend getting very annoyed because he was beating the hell out of our amps trying to bust them up, but the sound just kept coming through. Marc and Pete Townshend never hit it off. In fact, Townshend used to be a bit of a bastard! The only two guys who were okay were John Entwhistle and Keith Moon, who used to hang out with us and have a laugh [later on, in fact, Marc would interview Keith Moon for Thames TV's *Today*, shown on 29th September 1975]. The only problem with Keith was that he'd smash up the hotel rooms to such an extent that we were

Marc in his John's Children days, 1967.

always on the move to alternative hotels — he was an absolute lunatic!

'Marc wasn't a very good musician, but he suited John's Children perfectly, because when he went on stage he was something else! Not being a very good musician didn't really matter, that was the way the songs were structured anyway. Marc did used to get very heavily drunk though, and sometimes we had to tell him to stop drinking before a show. I mean, there were one or two gigs we did where he was just too out of it — a whole bottle of red wine before going on stage!

'Marc never had any aspirations to work with anyone "famous", not around the John's Children time, anyway. I think he always wanted to go it alone. John's Children was something that appealed to him at the time and it possibly took him into a different direction, but it certainly wasn't going to be a long term thing for him. We all felt in the band that he was only using us for a short period of time. We brought him in because he was a good songwriter and because we all thought he was a lot better than Geoff McClelland, who we chucked out.

'Our whiter-than-white image came out of Simon Napier-Bell's head. He had this idea that we would be very cherubic and innocent off stage, but that when we came out on stage, we would be exactly the opposite. At this time, Marc was still into his "folk" thing, even though he was involved with this crazy electric band. He was *very* into Bob Dylan's 'Blonde On Blonde' album. He was forever playing it to us round Simon's flat. I can't remember anything else that inspired Marc so much as Dylan.

'None of us were on retainers, although we were taken everywhere by limousines, stayed in the best hotels, and given good meals and a certain amount of pocket money (not very much, though!) We didn't make any money from the records because we'd spent so much on other things.

'There wasn't any animosity when Marc decided to do his own thing, because we didn't actually split up, we just sort of drifted apart. When we returned from Germany we had all our gear confiscated, so we couldn't actually do anything — in this interim period Marc got together with some other guy and started to write and play acoustic guitar. We were deported from Germany, Simon was losing interest in us, etc., etc., that's when Marc decided to go and do something else.

'I never thought that Marc had that "superstar" quality about him at the time. I was amazed when he made it so big. I thought he was quite boring in his John's Children period. Maybe we helped to bring out his more extrovert character years later.

'I did, in fact, listen to Tyrannosaurus Rex and thought it was horrible stuff. I thought T.Rex were great though. He played the pop star and made instant throwaway records which were brilliant. I thought, "He's back to how he should have been." I think he would have still been doing it now, had he lived. He would've been up there with all the new bands.

'I don't think Marc ever improved his guitar playing. Even with John's Children, I don't remember Marc ever practising with his guitar. He'd prefer to write, or read his strange books. I suppose his vivid imagination and what he used to read helped him enhance his songwriting.

'It was funny seeing him later on, playing the guitar hero, but then again he was just acting — he couldn't really do it. He did make it work though. He was a pastiche of all those heavy metal axe players.

'I didn't see Marc again for years until one day in 1977. I was running down the King's Road in Chelsea, late for rehearsals, and this Mini tooted at me, the window wound down and it was Marc and his girlfriend Gloria. He asked me what I was doing and I told him that I was on my way to rehearse with my band, Radio Stars. Then he said, "Well, I've got a television show coming up soon and you must come and do it — I'll give you a ring in a few weeks time." To my amazement, he did — so Radio Stars appeared on *Marc* [see pages 102–3]. After the show we arranged to meet up and go out for a meal, but it never transpired because sadly Marc had the accident — so I never saw him again.

'Marc has really left his stamp on rock music. Just as much as Buddy Holly, Jimi Hendrix and the like.'

MICKEY FINN INTERVIEW

On this rare occasion in November, 1974 Mickey Finn was interviewed, shortly before the Agora Club gig in Ohio, USA. This is what he had to say:

Do you resent having to play 'Bang A Gong' and 'Jeepster' at every concert?

M: No, not at all. I mean, I really get off playing 'Bang A Gong' — it's very much part of us.

Were the first electric concerts booed like the Dylan ones?

M: Not really, because the fans expected a progression in that field. It's the only way we could have gone — we couldn't have gone on just doing folk things — for our own heads, as well as everybody elses.

So many of the rock people in Britain are leaving because of the tax situation. Are you contemplating any kind of a move, or have you made one?

M: Yeah, we've bought homes in France as well as over here.

Last year you did a number of dates with Three Dog Night. Do you feel like you really got across to the type of Americans who are basically an AM radio type crowd?

M: Basically I think Three Dog Night have a pop audience anyway, they're very hip orientated like we are. I think we come across very well, it was a very good tour.

Are you pleased with the way the American TV has presented you? Does British TV treat you any better?

M: British TV hasn't got as many channels or outlets, there's only about two shows that I can think of, one of which we won't do and another one, called Top Of The Pops, which is singles orientated and only covers the Top Twenty/Thirty.

What was the show that you wouldn't do?

M: The Old Grey Whistle Test.

Mickey and Marc.

What do you really feel that T.Rex has to do to conquer American audiences? Do you think more of an AM type thing?

M: I think more FM now — we're definitely an LP band.

Would you like T.Rex mania to hit the States like it did in Britain?

M: No. I think the States is a vast country — you're known on the East Coast but not on the West Coast, or vice versa, but I feel that we should come here much more than we do.

How has T.Rex mania changed in England over the past year or two, if at all?

M: We've done six or seven dates in England, which were just crazy, like we never stopped.

Do you feel rock in general is starting to stagnate?

M: Yes, in lots of ways. I don't think there's much direction rock-wise.

How do you rate people like Eno and Bryan Ferry?

M: Bryan Ferry covers old tunes by The Platters and things. He's okay, but I don't think he's anything to go crazy about.

Do you have any criticism of American audiences in general?

M: No, I dig them, I really dig them.

What impressions have you got from this tour? Are the audiences relating more to the group?

M: Very difficult to say, because I'm not in the audience, but the reaction has been very good.

What would be the next step for you if it all just ended? Would you be content to stay in music, or content in some other field, like art?

M: Personally, I'd like to write and do an LP or something, and I'd quite like to do some acting as well.

Do you have any influences?

M: I quite like the congo players in Curtis Mayfield's band.

What's it like working with Bolan?

M: It's pretty well smooth, we get on very well.

Can you tell me anything about the next LP? [Light Of Love]

M: It's turned out really fantastic.

Do you feel you're treated better now by Casablanca than Warner Bros.? Have you got a better deal from them?

M: I don't know yet, it's too early. We've only been with them a few months.

Are you going to have a new single out soon?

M: Yes, it's called 'Zip Gun Boogie', but, that will be a little while yet.

Is that going to be just for USA or world-wide?

M: That will probably be released in Europe.

Would you rather play to an audience that gets really excited, or one that just sits and listens?

M: I really do believe in giving out what you're getting back — exchange of energies. There's nothing worse if we're rocking and nobody's reacting. I really do like people to get it on and bang a gong, to coin a phrase.

Do you think there's any chance of releasing the 'T.Rex Great Hits' LP in America?

M: It's difficult, really, because most of the singles haven't been released here — there's not much to relate to, but maybe later on.

'Zinc Alloy' seemed like a drastic change to the other records. Were people really enthusiastic about it in England?

M: Yes, people dug the LP ever such a lot. I like it very much. You've got to realise that one has to change — I mean, not only are you expected to change, you *have* to change.

I really appreciate you giving your time like this.

M: No problem at all.

THE MIKE MANSFIELD INTERVIEW

'I first met Marc in the mid 60's, when I was doing a show at Granada TV produced by Muriel Young. I can't remember what it was called. Marc sang one of his very early songs and even then I thought how outrageous he was. He looked pretty extravagant and his performance was over the top. That's what was always nice about him. It was a solo performance, no musicians and he was dressed in a red velvet suit — absolutely true! — and he had very heavy make-up on as well.

'We were always friends. He lived in a house off the Fulham Road [Holmead Road] and we used to go to a restaurant just around the corner. That's when he was living with Gloria Jones. We used to see each other in Chelsea and in Morton's Club, in Berkeley Square. I was with him in Morton's the week before he died. We were talking about doing a new show together. Marc said "Let's meet up and have a drink", so we went to Morton's. That was the last time I saw him. He told me that he wanted to do a "pop opera" — not a rock opera, because he wasn't really rock 'n' roll — well, he was a bit rock 'n' roll, but he was also a harmony of contrasts, a mixture of all kinds of things. He wanted it to be on television first, and then on stage. He was full of plans like that; that was the purpose of our meeting at that time, to discuss this pop opera. It was going to include a whole batch of newly-written songs — he was *always* playing me new songs. Marc was always so excited and interested in what I thought about them, for no other reason than that I was a friend, and he knew that I would say if I didn't like anything.

'Marc did every *Supersonic*, in that every time he had a new record out he would be on. He wanted to be on and I wanted him on. The game was always, "What are we going to do with you, Marc?"

'I can remember once we tied him onto a sort of extraordinary pneumatic lift that came up out of nowhere — he loved all that. Then he would be on the end of a crane swishing around the studio — he was as over-the-top as I was, that's why it all worked. We both gelled. If I'd say, "We're going to blow you up this week, Marc", he'd have loved that. In fact, he'd say to *me*, "Are you going to blow me up this week?" — he really did! The more access to excess he had, the happier he

Right: Gloria, Mike and Marc at a fancy-dress party held at Mike Mansfield's home in Wimbledon, 1976.

was. *Supersonic* was recorded, so I'd just let Marc do what he wanted to. I'd always know that I could catch him with a camera. I would always say, "Go wherever you want to go, do whatever you want to do" — which is different to how they do pop shows on television now. Today artists are "set" in concrete, just go in and come out — nobody ever moves on television anymore. I would always construct sets for the kind of acts we would have on *Supersonic* and allow them to walk or run along walkways that you could see through underneath — Marc was always very good at that. He was an extraordinarily lyrical performer, in movement as well as in music and song. His movement was an extension of what he sang. Each week on *Supersonic* we would do something special for somebody — usually the people who copped it were Gary Glitter, or Marc, or Midge Ure (when he was in Slik). Marc was a kind of "Rosetti" type of person: he loved lyrical things.

'I would usually say when we booked him what we were going to do, and the more we did to him, the more he liked it. When we said that we were going to do "Ride A White Swan" and carve out this enormous swan out of polystyrene and he was going to have to stand in it and glide around the studio (the swan was built around a fork-lift truck and came with a funny little driver!), Marc couldn't wait and got very excited about the idea. I also told him that we were going to drop a ton of feathers on top of him during the performance — when we dropped feathers on *Supersonic*, it wasn't just a bag of it, it *was* almost a ton of it!

'The day after *Supersonic* they were filming the TV programme *Upstairs, Downstairs* in the same studio; during one of the more "tender" moments in one of the scenes, some of the leftover feathers began slowly falling from the ceiling . . . We sometimes went too far!

'We once got hold of an empty water-tank and said to Marc, "We're going to fill it up with foam while you're singing 'Dreamy Lady' ". By the end he was completely smothered in ten feet of foam! (I got the idea originally from the Rolling Stones video, "It's Only Rock 'n' Roll".) If ever a show was made for an artist or an artist was made for a show, it was *Supersonic* and Marc.

'One thing that he always wanted to do that we never did (but would have, had the chance arisen and the song been right) was to go on Kirby wires around the studio. He always wanted to do that. He would have made a wonderful Peter Pan — in fact, he *was* Peter Pan.

'Marc once gave me his Bel-Ami jukebox stacked full of Marc Bolan records — it's in my house in Wimbledon and in working order. I always found Marc to be a

Gloria, Britt Ekland, Marc and Rod Stewart at a party to promote the release of Rod's album 'A Night on the Town', 1976. In an interview at this time, Rod commented: 'He's great, old Bolan, but he's always giving me his clothes! He gave me a scarf saying it would really suit me, then a pair of gloves saying *they'd* suit me . . . I'm ending up with all his old clothes! I remember him coming to a party of mine once; he was sick all over the floor and ended up having to sleep in my bath. His girlfriend, Gloria, stormed out—she was really annoyed.' [Told to Syd Jerram—a friend of Caron's—who met Rod Stewart in Birmingham on his 1976 tour, during an interview with Syd's friend Paul Morley.]

very generous person, in the spiritual as well as in the materialistic sense. I mean, anyone who gives someone a jukebox has to be a generous person. People don't do that very often, not to me anyway. I mean, it's the first and only time it's happened.

'He was a star. They don't make people like Marc Bolan anymore, and certainly there's no contemporary artist around like him today. He was totally and completely an original and an individual. He had an incredible talent — goodness knows where it would've gone and how it would've developed had he lived.

'He loved the *theatre* of rock. I can remember him going on about how much he admired David Bowie. Marc's home was very theatrical. I recall that he was very much into the colour red, especially in his house in Holmead Road — he had splashes of red everywhere.

'I saw Marc at his most vulnerable, because there was a time when he wasn't as popular and successful as he could or should have been. We carried on, as this didn't matter to me — because we had a kind of deal between the two of us. I could do anything I wanted to do on the show, and it was exposure for him, which was, hopefully, keeping him buoyant (on TV and selling records) because the one vital thing for a star is to be seen.

'In the business I am in, I do of course receive many records and I did get all Marc's as well, although I would've bought them anyway, because I did like the songs.

'The very last *Supersonic* went out with a bang, with Marc taking the lead. There was a cast of thousands: Gloria Jones, John Lodge, Alvin Stardust, Dave & Ray Davies, Justin Hayward and Elkie Brooks. Not a bad line-up . . .

'Marc also did videos with us and Eric Hall for EMI. We finished at least two of them, although I can't remember the songs. We also did some songs that we didn't use for the show; they're about somewhere.

'Marc invited Hilary to Abbey Road studios in September, shortly before the accident. He was working with Gloria, putting down brass tracks for some new project. Whatever happened to that I don't know.

'After that terrible, terrible car crash I went to the hospital to see Gloria and she didn't know that Marc had died. She was lying there with her jaw all wired up, unaware of the tragedy. It wasn't until a few days later that she was told that Marc had died.

'It was quite a good way for him to go. If you're a big pop star or film star, like Marilyn, or James Dean, and you've got to go, the best way of staying alive is to die young. There's nothing as tired as an old rock star. As Marc said, he never thought that he'd reach thirty. He was very mystical, a man of many colours. There were lots of Marc Bolans, actually.

'I went to Marc's funeral with Hilary and Muriel Young. Everyone was there: David Bowie, Rod Stewart, Steve Harley and all. It was extraordinary. That was like a pop opera — so maybe he got his pop opera in the end, after all . . .!'

3. 'NO RENT TO PAY,
LANDLORD'S A QUEEN . . .'

The following pages contain a selection of short stories, poems, drawings and various notes spanning the twelve-year period from 1964 to 1976.

All of the items included in this chapter have remained, until now, officially unpublished; we have decided to print them here as they are excellent examples of the extent to which Marc's creativity was expressed in ways other than through his music. They also show Marc's distinctive sense of humour — an important aspect of his life and writings that should not be forgotten.

One of the most interesting items in this section is the extract from Marc's diary, written in 1966 and entitled (in his own words) 'A Bitova Diary'. The original manuscript is, unfortunately, in such poor condition that it is unsuitable for direct reproduction, so we have transcribed it here word for word. The only alterations we have made have been in the interest of reader-friendliness — by which we mean that, although it is a *verbatim* copy of the original, some words and names (such as 'Epstein', 'Knightsbridge', 'lighthouses', 'bossanova' etc.) which, due to his dyslexia, Marc had misspelt, have been corrected.

From reading 'A Bitova Diary' it is easy to picture Marc's way of life at the time, his dress sense and the places he frequented. This was also a period when he was very influenced by Bob Dylan; so much so that Marc began using his own version of 'street writing', which eventually produced some very evocative passages.

The material has been collected from various sources: some of the manuscripts were given to Caron by Marc himself, others were donated to us by Simeon and Phyllis Feld, several were given by friends and a few obtained at various auctions of pop memorabilia over the past ten years.

CHARING X ROAD

A short story written by Marc under the name Toby Tyler in 1964.

I'm walking down Charing X, digging the pavement, and speaking to Cadilacs, nose pressed against a bookshop window, hung up cos' there's so much knowledge in there, yet so little out here. I smile secretly as I kick a tin can along the sidewalk, farting in the wind and wishing to have a real crazy scene, but nothing happens. Meet some American tourists, make like a jerk and squeeze £2, and laugh cos' unknown to them I spoke with an American accent. Time it goes, I'm still walking the dog. Meet a woman like Jeanne Moreau and I chat. She says I'm pretty but too young. I say nobody puts me down like that, and storm off. I wanted her. Talk to some more Cadilacs and dance with some real hung-up dustbins, even some people too, but by 9 o'clock I'm still walking down Charing X Road.

— Toby Tyler

HUNG UP, WINDOW WATCHIN'

Handwritten poem by Marc, 1965.

3.   : hung up, window watchin,

I sit, lookin outa my window,
thinkin how hung up, people are
                                    lookin
but say theys lookin straight
back & thinkin, I's hung up too.

If I was jesus and an I'mortal god,
I'd make bridget Bardo, sleep
                                    with me.
I'd swing on my heels, I pull down
                                    jails
and drive an aston Martin, but
thats I'f I was jesus and I'aint
    So its back to my soapbox.

RIGGS O'HARA

Story/poem written under the name Marc Feld in 1966, about an American actor friend.

Walking down the highway strolling and singing, singing a song that made me laugh, about a sewer near a park, about a dog who couldn't bark.

 After a while I get very weary, and stop to take a rest. When up walks a cool looking hipster all togged up in a dirty grey vest. He told me he was a folk singer, I said I was one too. Soon we had a long cool chat, and eventually became as thick as glue. We wrote many poems and stories, of which this is one. We sang lots of crazy folk songs, blazing in the pale warm afternoon sun. My friend's name I cannot tell you, I promised him I would not say, but eventually he became an actor, and acted in a play, hope I'm a dustbin singer someday.

 P.S. I can't keep a secret, his name was Riggs O'Hara — he was a yank.

— Marc Feld
Written 12 o'clock pm (Midnight in bed)

A BITOVA DIARY

For the first time today I'm feeling good, and maybe I should. I just took aspirins, I'm high flying. When I woke this morning my head felt like the blast had happened in my brain, you know the pain could drive a guy insane. So anyway, I make my way to the kitchen, which ain't hard when it's the only other room you got going for yer. So I get out my crapo cornflakes and a couple of ill-looking eggs with no lion on them — he must have escaped, he got wise to me, I don't dig lion. I make some ploppy coffee, I have a fight with the breakfast — I'm a born loser.

 I throw on a pair of Levi's and a denim jerkin, and make for uptown. Got no loot so I can't jump a bus, so I hitch a lift — only 'I' can get picked up by the only 97-year-old granny-type nymph in Tooting, man I tell you they were down to her knees. Anyway, after fighting off Lady Chatterly, I get off at Charing X — how come everybody's rich

Marc, 1966.

but me? I walk round the 'Dilly for an hour — nobody tries to pull me — oh no, not another off day. I'd brought my guitar along, so I busk awhile, nothing happens, so where's Brian Epstein then? I make 7/6d, so I stroll over to the Wimpey and have a coke, man where did all the queens go? Feeling down, talking of down, I'm down to my last 1/-. Maybe I'll get some scenes in Knightsbridge. So I jump a tube and ride off into the underground kingdom of London Transport, the only place where the negro is top dog. When I come out of darkly Africa, it's raining, so I wait awhile. You see lots of E types and things here you know, kinda posh. See a chick I know, so I flag her down. Hey girl I say, got any bread. She's awful pretty, got long straw-like hair and high flying cheek-bones, full red lips and big huge breasts, and lovely legs. Man you know I reckon if I had a lion on me, I'd be a poet. She says she thought I was Donovan, that's why she showed out. Something brings me down more than others mothers (hey that rhyme) slime, (dog) bog. So feeling real squishy I leave Knightsbridge and head for my penthouse suite in Upper Tooting.

Feeling good I slip on my levi's and have a glass of wine (P.S. one glass of wine and I'm anybody's). I put some sounds on the player and do my yoga exercises, yes I bet you weren't hip to me being a yogurt. The 'phone rings, it's a friend who's arranged a gig. Where? A pub in Chelsea — not bad. So I wash and put my boots on, and I sing a song about a bow-legged prostitute whose name was Fred.

The gig's not bad, I got £3 and four meat pies. So next morning I went on a shopping spree. I bought strings, a new Kazoo and harp, and a Jesse Fuller album (San Francisco Bay Blues) — he's a gas.

Next three days spent digging the album and learning the songs.

I also went shopping and saw a guy who looked just like Jesus, and (I swear on my dirty underwear) he winked at me knowingly.

Broke again, still at least I've no rent to pay (landlord's a queen). I get stoned and think I'm Harold Wilson in his caveman aspect and I'm catching dinosaurs and beating my chest in leopard-skin briefs from John Stevens, and that while doing my tarzan croon, I swallow my pipe. Just then the postman knocks and I wake up to the world and scream that I'm really Ena Sharples in drag. It's only a bill so I burn it, then put the ashes in an ashtray and stick them on my Aunty Sady's ashes (God rest her nose). I write a song called 'Bossanova For Swinging Spastics' (and Andrew Oldham thinks *he's* sick). I steal the tune of the National Anthem — could be a hit. I go downstairs to the loo, only to see that the last person to do numbers didn't pull the chain, and it was floating about like a little ship. I was almost inspired to run upstairs and get my little duck and play lighthouses.

I make it to sleep and dream of going to Heaven, and seeing Big Daddy and having some scenes. You know when I get to them pearly gates, they were old and rusty and deserted. I made it through only to see weeds and darkness everywhere. When, then in the distance, I saw a huge temple of gold. I ran up but once more it was real rusty. Inside was much the same, must have been cool once upon a time, but now it was as if the great God of Heaven and Earth were dead and I hadn't noticed it before.

Every so often a big wind blew, as if calling to his Master to return. Guess it was a bad dream, maybe.

I didn't sleep too well last night, man that was a real spook dream, as if things ain't bad enough down here, without Jesus and his Dad pissing off and leaving us alone.

This morning I wash my hair — getting long and curled at the back. I look in the mirror, I see a young river God — his hair a-dripping and his body wet and fish-like. I dry my hair, I use the hoover, it's quicker. Wonder if I'm as beautiful today as I was yesterday. I slide down the castaway banisters and hurt my secret parts on the knob at the end. Now a break for another Marc Feld poem.

I ran into the sounds stark naked
Fearless, yet afraid, fearing, peering
into the pit of humanity
Screaming for my likeness to emerge
It was then I saw my GOD.

— Marc Feld
1966

to Rick Gretzk

15 Billings Rd

Fulham

S W 10

NOTTING HILL
10 OCT
1969

deep love
& some words
I hope you can
use
them
X
m

FOAMING BAYS

It seemed a nice way to start a day
Shipped in Sheba's Foaming Bay
A distant swimmer in a sea of trees
And then a bleached man with juggler's hands,
Scaled an oak to understand
The childlike sweetness in the sky's blue breeze.

Goddess in the fortress
Of the world is just a slaughteress
So let's grow into the sky
Just like a grove of trees

I danced thunderbound up to the mound
Of past and present pleasures found
All caged and guarded by the eyes of blind
River men with twisted limbs
Devised to choke the throats of kings
Robed in willow woven skins of hind.

— Marc Bolan
1968

Left and above: Handwritten envelope and poem sent by Marc to Rick Gretch of the group Family, October 1969. Another poem sent to Rick can be seen on the following page.

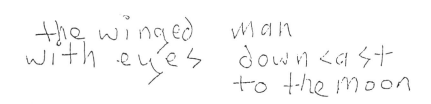

the winged man
with eyes downcast
to the moon

By the sound of Geyser Mound
The man with wings abides
On stormy nights free of frights
Children on his back ride.
From around his ears
Black herbal tears
Course darkly down his skull
In the bruised pale dawn
The infants yawn and their memorys are dulled
For the shaggered shape of the feathered man
Who limps to his eyrie of lavender
Could never fit within the maps and wit
Of the headlords who dictate
The childs' calender.

— Marc Bolan
1969

Above: Marc recited this poem on John Peel's radio show in 1969.

Right, top: Handbill advertising Marc's book of poetry, *The Warlock of Love* (Lupus, London: 1969). It sold over twenty thousand copies, making Marc one of England's biggest-selling poets!

Right, bottom: Marc's original working lyric for 'Girl', a track which finally appeared on his 1971 album 'Electric Warrior'.

GIRL

Girl, child of
the wind
you are
Child, girl as
a friend you are
beautifully kind
eternally mind you
are and me
as the same

are of you

Wind, child of the
one you are
Sun, how we
begun you know
beautifully kind
eternally fine
you are

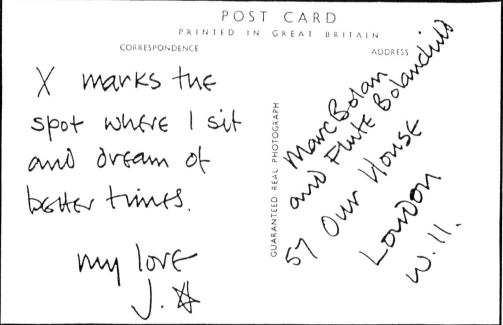

Above: Postcard to Marc from his wife June. '57 Our House' refers to 57 Blenheim Crescent in London's Notting Hill, where Marc and June lived for three years.

Right: Drawing by Marc.

unworshiped roman god

Above: Marc's handwritten 'Anniversary' message for possible inclusion in a pop magazine.

Right: Marc outside Radio London, 2nd September, 1972.

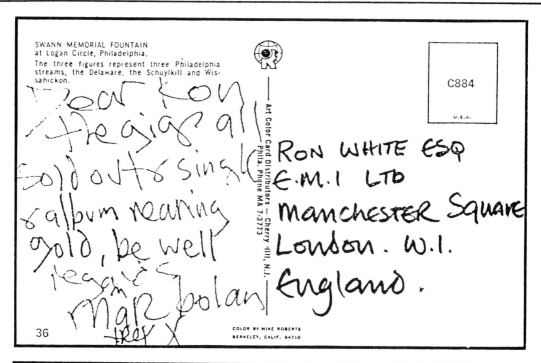

Above: handwritten postcards from Marc to EMI personnel concerning the 1972 tour of the USA and record sales.

Right: Drawing of woman by Marc, USA, 1974.

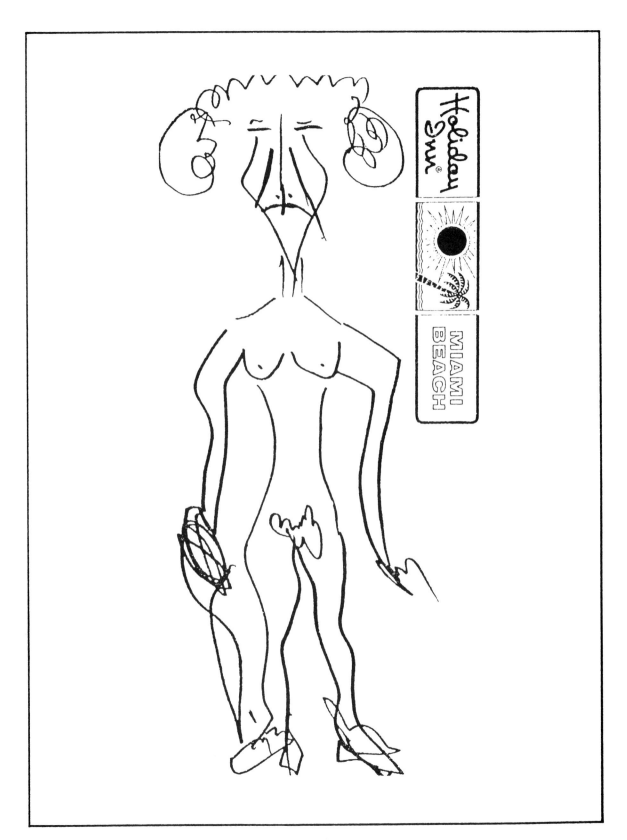

script idea ~~idea~~ battle ①

a group of post teens. rival gangs

3 boys . bolan, harley soft essex, nickolas soft
~~Roywood~~ bad
gang 1. gang 2

4 girls . gloria Dana one ~~Japanese~~
3 1 2

state/ el of each . who thru battle plays
gargian chess

short story use excalirbur as
basic idea .

1 day - as story - that ends
on leaving the flat &
met a rival gang ~~on~~ on
purple lawn outside their lift
same amout of kids, ~~bloody~~ bloody
fit Marz killed steve badly
knifed end on brain police magnicaling
all kids together & driving off in
a transparet plastic paddy wagon .

Original handwritten drafts by Marc for a futuristic story based on the medieval
legend of Excalibur. Marc's proposed cast would have included David Essex, Steve
Harley, Paul Nicholas, Gloria Jones, Dana Gillespie and Roy Wood. If Marc had

stategaurdian for orphan or ②
runaway kids, really a way to find
homes & ward for senile old folks.
at end of fight, they lock
each others gang in wagon
and go back to chess game
on blooded feild.
on feild only 3 corpses, marc
paul, & a cat.

| also |

as with marcs gang
~~&~~ davids gang to
first alltogether send
all takeing shower together
one shot gang - the another
will each elder read from
large old manuscript.

developed this and taken it further it might have proved a sideways step from his
renowned 'Children of Rarn' concept--a Tolkienesque story that Marc began writing
to music in 1967.

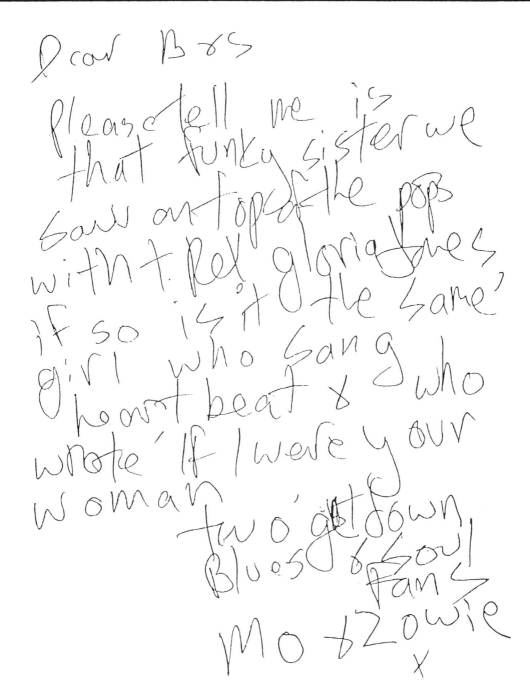

Dear B&S

Please tell me is
that funky sister we
saw on top of the pops
with t. Rex gloria jones
if so is it the same
girl who sang
heart beat & who
wrote 'If I were your
woman'
two o' get down
Blues & Soul
fans
Mo & Zowie
x

Left: Marc outside his house at 25 Holmead Road, Chelsea on 7th May, 1976.

Above: handwritten letter from Marc to *Blues and Soul* magazine, signed with the pseudonyms 'Mo and Zowie', 1975.

I need a cloak of
gold to live in
to veil my mind
from a ritting sun,
which one is for you to
decide upon,
a gaunlet, bold &
handsomley weilding
to & bruise the
faces of all wealthy
beggars, a pale man
am I, I own some
sky not all but only
a fool
would want
more

Left: handwritten poem by Marc, 1976.

Above, top: Marc outside his home in Holmead Road after a visit to the hairdresser, 3rd May, 1976. *Bottom:* Later the same day, Marc and Gloria leaving EMI House, Manchester Square, after a photo session. In the evening they went to see David Bowie in concert at Wembley, where they were seen dancing behind the stage.

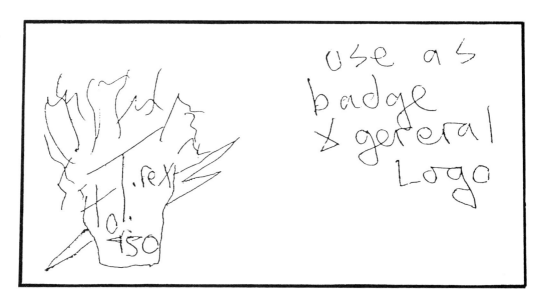

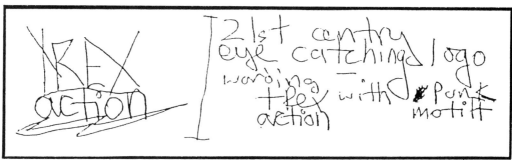

Above: Marc's designs for badge and logo during the beginning of his 1976 'punk period'. Neither design was ever used by Marc.

Right: Hand-drawn card to Gloria. Marc sometimes used to draw a smiling face alongside his signature, thus earning himself the nickname of 'Smiley'.

Gloria

I LOVE
YOU
from
Mark x

happy birthday to you from all of us

↑

I woke up this Morning
feeling rotten & Mean
Wondering if ill ever
find my teenage
Queen,

No

Left: Hand-drawn birthday card from Marc to Gloria on her thirty-first birthday
(19th October, 1976).

Above: Some scribbled verse by Marc, obviously feeling rather dejected at the
time!

4. 'I NEED TV WHEN I GOT T.REX' — MARC ON FILM

Marc was one of the few big pop performers of his generation who never really ventured into the world of 'serious' acting; unlike Mick Jagger, David Bowie or Phil Collins, Marc was exclusively a writer/musician. Even if he *had* fallen prey to the lure of the silver screen, it is doubtful whether he would have been very successful: he was too much of a *poseur*, too narcissistic to take on the mantle of any character other than that of his own self-created alter-ego.

However, it *was* of great importance that he should capture the essence of T.Rex in song and in performance. Marc used to tape himself on video or cassette as often as possible: at gigs, at home, anywhere. In fact he was one of the first people in England to own a video recorder.

There are, of course, literally hundreds of Marc's performances that have been available, at one time or another, on film or video around the world. To list them all would take a book in its own right so we have concentrated on those which relate to our own collection of unpublished photos, manuscripts and notes. The sections on 'Rollin' Bolan' and the 'Marc' shows were helped along by Caron's personal diaries and photos, as she was in attendance at the time.

Because Marc was one of the most visual performers of the '70s, it is essential to remember the many changes of image he underwent throughout the decade. For instance, the Glam Rock era (pretty-boy look with glitter); Zinc Alloy (metallic and heavy metal imagery); the Bolantino phase (short, slicked-back hair). Facts like these tend to get pushed aside, and, as a result, Bolan is pigeonholed in the Glitter Rock category alone. People forget that, although paving the way for the likes of Bowie, Gary Glitter, Sweet etc., Marc had disowned 'Glam Rock' by the end of 1973. Of course, with the aid of video, the many images of Marc can, thankfully, be watched and treasured forever.

Left: Mickey and Marc at the *Top of the Pops* studio, after performing 'Ride a White Swan', 1970.

```
                              16th November, 1971.


Marc Bolan Esq.,
31 Clarendon Gardens,
London, W.9.


Dear Marc,

        This is to confirm the appointments made
for the rest of the week.

Wed. 17th        3 pm.    Abner Stein
                          re: Book of Poetry
                          at: Charles Street.

Thurs. 18th    12 noon.   Iris Burton - Woman's Own
                          re: Article for Spring Issue
                          at: Clarendon Gardens.

Thurs. 18th      3 pm.    Ingrid Matthews and
                          Brian Lewis from A.T.V.
                          re: T.V. documentary on pop.
                          at: Charles Street.


        That's all for now.


                              Regards,



                              Marilyn.
```

Above: Letter to Marc from his secretary, Marilyn, confirming appointments: Wednesday, with literary agent to discuss the reissue of *The Warlock of Love*; Thursday, to be interviewed for magazine (the article, entitled 'Look What They've Done to Your Son, Ma', was eventually published in 1972); and for another filmed interview to be used in a TV documentary called *Whatever Happened to Tin Pan Alley?*, transmitted 28th March, 1972.

Right: Another letter to Marc from Marilyn, on Wizard letterhead, to arrange appearance to sing 'Telegram Sam' on *Top of the Pops*.

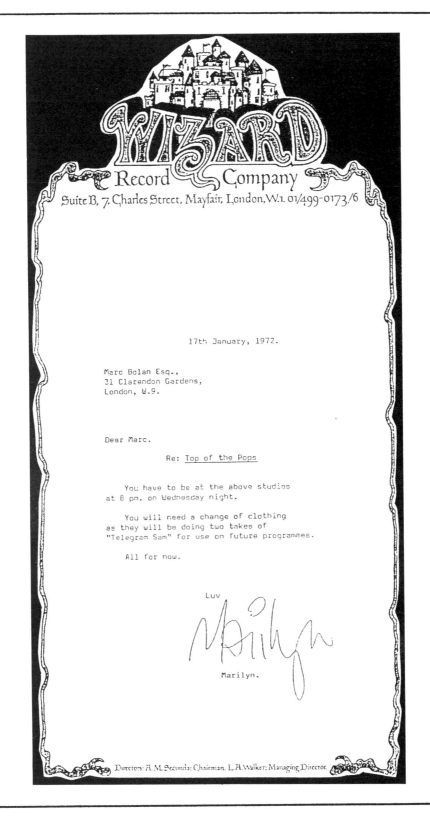

WIZARD Record Company

Suite B, 7, Charles Street, Mayfair, London, W.1. 01/499-0173/6

17th January, 1972.

Marc Bolan Esq.,
31 Clarendon Gardens,
London, W.9.

Dear Marc.

Re: Top of the Pops

    You have to be at the above studios
at 8 pm. on Wednesday night.

    You will need a change of clothing
as they will be doing two takes of
"Telegram Sam" for use on future programmes.

    All for now.

                    Luv

                    Marilyn.

Directors: A. M. Secunda: Chairman. L. A. Walker: Managing Director.

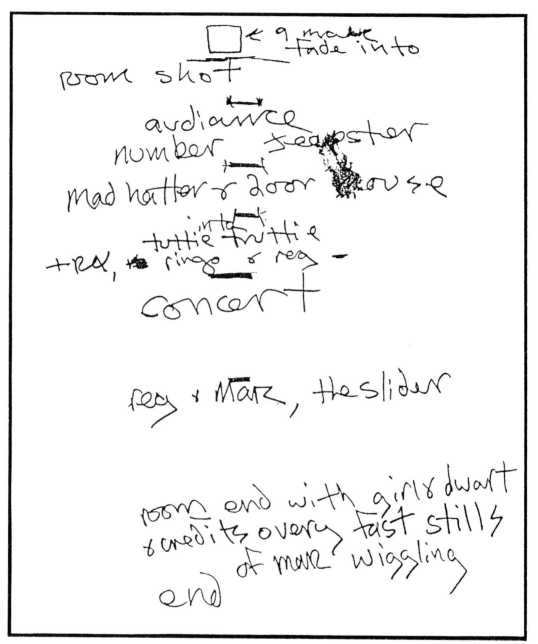

Above: Marc's handwritten notes for *Born to Boogie*.

Right: Performance at the Empire Pool Wembley, 18th March, 1972, for *Born to Boogie*.

Following pages: More notes for *Born to Boogie*. It appears that Marc wanted John Lennon to appear at one stage . . .

BORN TO BOOGIE

On 18 March 1972, T.Rex played two shows at the Empire Pool (now known as the Wembley Arena), attended by ten thousand fans. Both of these shows were filmed by the ex-Beatle, Ringo Starr; it was this footage that was to become the basis for the film, *Born To Boogie*.

The film was premièred on 14th December, 1972, at the Oscar One Cinema in Brewer Street, London. Unusually, the soundtrack album was not released at the same time, as Marc did not agree with what he saw as the 'reproduction of songs the fans must already have'. However, nearly twenty years on, the Marc Bolan Fan Club released the video of the film together with the soundtrack album, and *Born To Boogie* is now regarded as one of the great rock 'n' roll films of our time.

Unfortunately, there are various songs missing from the film, including 'The Slider', which was performed with Elton John. There is also dispute as to whether or not 'Rip It Up' was ever filmed/recorded, but it seems that Marc certainly intended it to be so, as can be seen from these handwritten notes. It was eventually released as the B-side to 'Think Zinc' in 1983.

nuns sing rip it up
its saturday nights
we just got payed,
fool about our money
dont try to save-
our hearts so gogo
have a time, cos
its saturdy nights
we feel fine

shot wild

Shot george
black & white in
cloak shot smiling
then slow motion
breaking colour &
have him poke out
tonge & have

a l

[T.Rex rings T.Rex rings T.Rex rings]

then into some
people like to rock
audeince & sound
track marc ringo talking
stoned rock & roll
lennon too

ROLLIN' BOLAN

In June 1976, London's Capital Radio announced that TV producer Mike Mansfield would be filming a series of concerts at the Wimbledon Theatre for a new LWT show called *Superpop*. T.Rex were one of the many groups appearing on Tuesday, 13th July, and tickets would be one pound each.

During the afternoon of the gig, Marc and the band arrived at the theatre for the soundcheck. Quite a lot of fans were already waiting there, and were able to meet Marc and get in to watch the soundcheck.

By 7 p.m. everyone was in their seats and waiting for the gig to start. Supporting Marc were three other singers and groups: the 60's singer, Leapy Lee, an acoustic trio called Laurie, Andrew & Zero, and the Australian band, AC/DC. Each of them played a short set.

Soon after AC/DC had finished, Marc, Steve Currie, Dino Dines, Davey Lutton and Miller Anderson walked on stage to loud cheers and screams from the audience. Miller was the new member of the group, who had only been seen before on *Top Of The Pops* (for 'I Love To Boogie') and was on second guitar and backing vocals.

Marc said that as they were filming for TV, they could not play very loud, so everyone would 'just have to pretend!'; T.Rex then went straight into the first number. This was 'I Love To Boogie', which was still high in the charts at the time; the song had to be played through twice because, as Marc explained, there had been a technical hitch during the first take.

Next came 'Funky London Childhood', which Marc introduced as being from 'the new album, due out any week' — up until now this song had only been heard on the TV programme, *Today* (in 1975), on a Capital Radio session and live on the 'Futuristic Dragon' tour, as it had not yet been released on record. Halfway through this performance the band had to stop and begin again with a second version; in the meantime Marc tuned up and played various guitar riffs.

Then came another unreleased song, 'The Soul Of My Suit', which again Marc announced as being from the new album. This, like 'Funky London Childhood', had only been heard live in 1975 and on a Capital Radio session, and was a much slower version than that which was eventually released as a single. Once again, after only a

Left: Two shots of Marc on *Rock On With 45*, after performing 'New York City'. The show was transmitted on 24th July, 1975.

Two snaps of Marc outside the Wimbledon Theatre in London on 13th July, 1976.

few lines, Marc had to stop due to feedback. During this break he started playing around with a flag given to him by a fan in the audience; then he thanked everyone for coming, said 'Don't forget you're on television!' and mentioned that the producer of *Top Of The Pops*, Robin Nash, was sitting on the balcony.

The technical faults took quite a long time to be sorted out, before Marc was able to continue with another version of 'The Soul Of My Suit'.

For the fourth song, 'New York City', Marc said, 'This is a song that was a hit for us about a year ago — I wrote it in the city of the stars'. This time there were no hitches and the band were able to complete the song in one take.

The final song was a new one, called 'Laser Love', which Marc said had not been recorded yet, but which would be the new single.

Once again, during this song, the band had to stop halfway through, this time because the guitars were going out of tune due to the heat from the TV lights. The second attempt had to be stopped for the same reason, so in the end they performed 'Laser Love' three times (during which the cameramen in the orchestra pit turned their cameras on the audience). As soon as they had finally finished, Marc bowed, said goodbye and left the stage.

This particular episode of *Superpop*, subtitled 'Rollin' Bolan', was transmitted on LWT at 10.45 p.m., 28th August 1976 (at present only available on video from the Marc Bolan Fan Club). Marc's part of the programme only lasted fifteen minutes; although the songs sounded great and it was well filmed, unfortunately all the song intros and 'talky bits' had been edited out.

Marc himself was out of the country when it was broadcast and had to have it videotaped for himself.

GET IT TOGETHER

On 22nd June, 1977, Marc and T.Rex appeared for the second time on Granada's pop show, *Get It Together*, this time to promote their new single, 'Dandy In The Underworld'.

On this occasion, Marc sang live to a pre-recorded backing track. He missed his cue on the first take, annoying the TV engineers some-what, but the second went well — so well, in fact, that it turned out to be one of Marc's finest TV appearances in years.

After the show, Marc caught a taxi to Piccadilly Station, where he boarded a train for London. During this journey home, he sat and talked about himself, saying things like, 'Marc Bolan and David Bowie are two of the biggest stars in England today, man ...' He would often refer to himself in the third person, as 'Marc Bolan', as if, for a while, he had slipped back into the reality of being plain old Mark Feld ...

[Both Marc's appearances on *Get It Together* can be seen as additional tracks on the *Marc* shows video — released 1988.]

Left: Photo session, Manchester, 1977, taken shortly before Marc's first appearance on *Get It Together*, where he sang 'Soul of my Suit'.

Above: Marc at Piccadilly Station, Manchester, after his second appearance on *Get It Together*.

Marc's handwritten ideas for one of the *Marc* shows, 1977.

THE *MARC* TV SHOWS

In August of 1977 it was officially announced that Marc would be given his own TV series called, appropriately enough, *Marc*. The six shows were to be recorded at the Granada TV studios in Manchester, and networked on all ITV channels on Wednesday afternoons, starting on August 24th at 4.20 p.m. (Granada's standard slot for pop shows). Marc, in his usual modest way, said, 'People have been clamouring for me to do a TV show for years — now I've finally given in.'

The original idea for the show came from Granada's Johnny Hamp, one of the first people to put The Beatles on TV in the 60's, who had wanted to create a rock/pop show that, in his own words, would 'bridge the gap between today and tomorrow, and generate a genuine feeling for young people.' However, it was the show's producer, Muriel Young, who suggested that Marc should be the presenter. Responsible for many of Granada's pop programmes, such as *Get It Together*, *Lift Off* and *The Arrows*, she had known Marc since he was fifteen when they had both been friends with the actor and writer Allen Warren.

It was decided that the format for the shows would be that Marc and the band would play three songs per show, with appearances by three guests (including one new artiste or group) and an all-girl dance group called Heart Throb. Marc planned to have as many of the genuinely talented New Wave bands on as possible — included in his list were The Stranglers, The Jam, The Boomtown Rats and The Damned — as well as some more established artists like Gary Glitter, Steve Harley and David Bowie; of course, not all of these made it onto the shows.

Marc had a whole set of clothes designed and made specially for the shows, all done by Colin Wilde, which included a gold brocade top, a leopard-skin suit and a pink satin tie-up top with the name 'Marc' across the front. And, on the week of the first show, the *TV Times* featured a full-page colour photo of Marc, together with a short article.

Show One

The first show opened with what would be the theme song for the series, a brand-new track called 'Sing Me A Song', which played over the opening titles, before the camera moved onto Marc and the band (at the time consisting of Dino Dines, Tony Newman and Herbie Flowers).

During the show Marc would also perform 'I Love To Boogie', 'Jeepster' and the then-new single 'Celebrate Summer' (despite several plays on the shows, this would fail to get into the charts) while The Jam played their single, 'All Around The World'. At the end Marc closed this (and every) show with the words, 'Keep a little Marc in your heart, and watch the same Marc time, the same Marc channel'.

Show Two

This time Marc and the band opened with 'Celebrate Summer', surrounded by a team of skateboarders, followed by 'Ride A White Swan', in which Marc wore sunglasses that had pictures of the sky projected onto them, and finished with a fast version of the old '50s rock 'n' roll song, 'Endless Sleep'. Alfalpha were one of the guest groups; managed by Marc's friend Jeff Dexter, they had worked on the 'Dandy In The Underworld' album.

Show Three

'Groove A Little', 'Hot Love' and a cover of the Chris Montez song, 'Let's Dance', were the three T.Rex songs played on this show; among the guests were The Boomtown Rats, performing their first single, 'Looking After Number One' (helped, incidentally, by Heart Throb, who completely lost their routine during the song) and Hawkwind, who Marc introduced as his 'best friends'. Their singer, Bob Calvert, sported a stuffed hawk on his wrist, for which Granada had had to send out specially.

Show Four

The fourth show featured 'New York City', another version of 'Endless Sleep', and, to end the show, 'Dandy In The Underworld', which Marc sang live. The only guest of interest was The Steve Gibbons Band, although there was also an obscure video of Queen's Roger Taylor, singing his solo single, 'Testify'.

Show Five

During this show, Marc was reunited with his old friend from John's Children, Andy Ellison (see pages 45–9), who was appearing with his new band, Radio Stars (Marc had invited Andy onto the show after a chance meeting on the King's Road). The three T.Rex songs were 'Sing Me A Song', 'Celebrate Summer' and 'Get It On'.

Marc and Radio stars at the Granada TV Studios, August, 1977.

Show Six

The day of this recording was beset with problems — almost everything seemed to go wrong. To start with, Generation X arrived late, due to a breakdown on the motorway; then, because of studio problems, they had to record their song five times, with Marc repeating the introduction each time. For a while things seemed to go a little more smoothly, as Marc did an electric version of 'Debora', followed by 'Ride A White Swan' (a repeat from Show Two). Then David Bowie, Marc's main guest that week, sang his new single, 'Heroes' (according to Marc, it was Bowie's own idea to appear on the show).

By now, however, time was pressing: the studio closed at seven and Marc, Bowie and the band had still to record the final song. Finally though, Marc said his

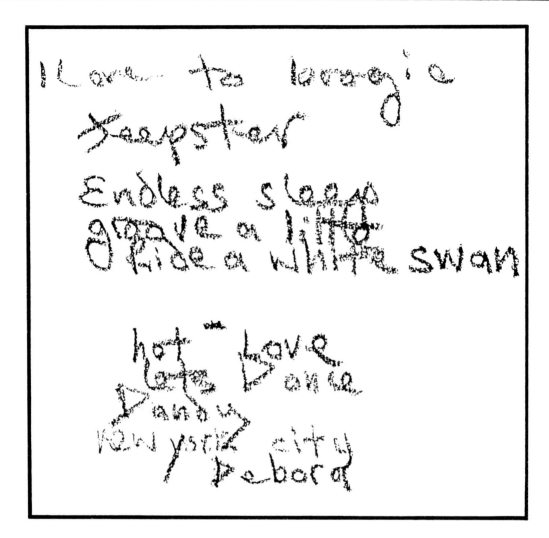

Handwritten list of songs to be featured on the *Marc* shows.

goodbyes and went into 'Standing Next To You' (a debatable title, as Bowie had sung 'sitting next to you' in rehearsal) with Bowie on guitar and vocals. Fifty seconds into the song came the final disaster: Marc fell off the stage ... As there was no more studio time left, this had to be the final take and Marc's tumble would have to be preserved for posterity.

Naturally Marc was very upset about the final song, as well as some of the other events of the day, but while watching the playback with Bowie, he realised that, despite the apparent shambles, there was still a good show in there.

With fans after recording one of the *Marc* shows, August/Sept., 1977.

The whole series was very successful; on the strength of this, Marc went into negotiations for a second series, of thirteen shows this time, which would have gone out in 1978. It is clear from Marc's notes that he had plenty of ideas. These included doing duets with Steve Harley on 'Dandy In The Underworld' and with Gary Glitter on 'Little Darling', getting The Vibrators to sing 'London Girls', T.Rex playing 'Telegram Sam' and Marc, Gloria and the band singing 'We'll Meet Again' at the end of the last show.

Exactly three years after, because of endless requests from Marc's fans, Granada repeated the *Marc* shows at the same time on Wednesday afternoons, although now the six episodes were condensed down to five, and omitted several guests and two T.Rex songs — 'Get It On' and 'Celebrate Summer'.

Above: Marc reading fan-mail and signing autographs at the office of his publicist, Keith Altham, September, 1977.

Right: Tyrannosaurus Rex programme, 1968. Note the name at the bottom of the bill!

5. 'IN SHEER DAZZLING RAIMENT'
— MARC ON TOUR

From 1968–77, Marc toured extensively almost every year, taking in several countries throughout the world, i.e., England, Germany, France, Japan, the USA, Australia, Sweden, Norway, Canada etc.

In 1976, Caron and a group of friends decided to hire a minibus to follow T.Rex on the 'Futuristic Dragon' British tour: seventeen gigs in total, which covered an area from Folkestone in Kent, to Glasgow, Scotland. During the tour, she met Marc almost every day (they had first met after a gig at Tiffany's nightclub, Great Yarmouth in July 1975 and at dates thereafter throughout the '75 tour) and he became very friendly towards their group, chatting to them after gigs on many occasions, and even treating them to the odd meal. By the end of the tour he knew them all by

FOR THE LION AND THE UNICORN
IN THE OAK FORESTS OF FAUN

ROY GUEST
presents

TYRANNOSAURUS REX
in concert
with
JOHN PEEL
and
VYTAS SERELIS—SITAR
and
DAVID BOWIE—MIME

No smoking in the Auditorium. The taking of photographs in the Auditorium is not permitted.

A NEMS ENTERPRISE

2/6

TOWN HALL · BIRMINGHAM
Telephone 236 2392
SATURDAY, 15th FEBRUARY at 8.00 p.m.
Tickets:　　15/-　　12/6　　10/-　　7/6　　5/-
from Town Hall Box Office and usual agents

for the lion
and the unicorn
in
the oak forest
of faun

Tyrannosaurus Rex

in concert with

John Peel

and friends

A
NEMS
PRESENTATION

HIP
CNO
SIS

HASTINGS PRINTING CO., DRURY LANE, ST. LEONARDS-ON-SEA, SUSSEX Hastings 2450

Left: Handbill promoting Tyrannosaurus Rex concert, 1969. *Above:* Cover of 1969/70 tour programme signed by Marc and Mickey Finn, who had just replaced Steve Peregrine Took. The band was on tour to promote their forthcoming album 'A Beard of Stars', released on 22nd March, 1970.

SATURDAY, FEBRUARY 26, 1972 -- BOSTON

ENTIRE GROUP
Cleveland to Boston:

Later flight.

Leave: Cleveland, Ohio   11:25 AM United #438
Arrive: Boston, Mass.   12:51 PM
                                       2.00pm.

Greyhound bus will transport group to hotel

HOTEL: Holiday Inn
                1651 Mass.
                Cambridge, Mass. 02138
                617/491-1000

GARY STROMBERG -- MARC open for press via TONY SECUNDA

T. REX ROOMS:

1. Tony Secunda _ _ _ _ _ single   *1.30) HOTEL*
2. Marc Bolan   single   *2.30) Interviews*
3. Mickey Finn _ _ _ _ _ single   *3.30)*
4. Steve Curry   double
5. Bill Legend _ _ _ _ _ double
6. Mike O'Harloran   double
7. Mickey Marmalade _ _ double
8. Mickey Thomas   double/Rolling Stone
9. Keith Morris _ _ _ _ double/Photographer

WARNER BROS. PERSONNEL:

10. Carl Scott   single
11. Bob Regehr   single
12. Russ Shaw   single
13. Gary Stromberg   single
14. Bill Shumow   single

5:00 PM   Sound Check - T. REX

DATE: Fenway Theatre
                Boston, Mass.
                2 shows - 7:30 PM & 10:00 PM

Above: Hotel details for T. Rex and entourage, Boston, Mass., on 26th February, 1972. The band was on tour to promote the 'Electric Warrior' album, and to try generally to raise the band's profile in the USA.

Right: Marc on stage at Newcastle City Hall, 24th June, 1972.

name and became a kind of distant friend: during the 1977 tour in France, the group ran out of money — Marc booked all five of them into a hotel for the night, even paying the bill. Later that year they repeated their trek around Britain for the 'Dandy In The Underworld' tour, when Caron became friends with Marc's girlfriend, Gloria Jones, and his manager, Tony Howard. She kept a daily diary of these events, which, together with new photographs, forms the backbone of this chapter about Marc's life on the road. It makes interesting reading and reveals the truth about certain incidents; for instance, when Marc claimed that a champagne bottle thrown through his dressing room window had cut his wrist. The truth about this and other stories is contained within . . .

Left: Cover of the official tour programme, 1972. The tour dates were as follows: 9th June—Birmingham Odeon; 10th June—Cardiff Capital; 16th June—Manchester Belle Vue; 24th June—Newcastle City Hall.

Below: Marc in concert on the 1975 tour, a short series of dates in the UK: 13th July—Palace Lido, Isle of Man; 23rd July—Tiffany's, Great Yarmouth; 25th July—Pier Pavilion, Hastings; 26th July—Leas Cliffe Hall, Folkestone (where photo below was taken).

These were really warm-up gigs for the upcoming 'Futuristic Dragon' tour, and among the songs played were 'Jeepster', '20th Century Boy', 'Teenage Dream', 'Telegram Sam', 'Zip Gun Boogie', 'New York City', 'The Soul of My Suit', 'Hot Love' and 'Get It On'. (Although Marc was featuring 'The Soul of My Suit' this track was not released until 12th March, 1977).

THE FUTURISTIC DRAGON TOUR — 1976

In 1976, T.Rex began their longest tour of the UK for five years, comprising eighteen dates in total. Marc had planned the tour to coincide with the release of the new album, 'Futuristic Dragon'.

The line-up consisted of: Marc (vocals and guitar), Steve Currie (bass), Dino Dines (keyboards), Davey Lutton (drums), Gloria Jones (clavinet and backing vocals) and Tyrone Scott (keyboards and backing vocals). A large, green, cardboard dragon with flashing eyes and smoking nostrils was used as the backdrop throughout the tour.

The first date was at the Central Hall, Chatham, Kent on 5th February. Before the gig Marc and the band decided to go out for a Chinese meal at the appropriately named Two Dragons restaurant. A group of us talked to Marc inside, where he spoke about the tour and signed photos (see photos opposite).

Marc in concert at the Central Hall, Chatham, Kent, on the first day of the 'Futuristic Dragon' tour, 5th February, 1976.

Marc and Gloria signing autographs together with (*top*) Tony Howard (Marc's manager) and (*bottom*) Arthur Max (a lighting engineer) at the Two Dragons Restaurant, Chatham, 5th February, 1976.

A friend of mine, Alf Bradley, asked Marc if he would be performing 'The Soul Of My Suit', as the song had been written over a year ago but remained unreleased. Marc said that he had forgotten about the song but would consider recording it in the future (in fact, it was eventually released in 1977). He then sang, unaccompanied, a whole verse from the song, much to our delight.

Later that evening Marc and T.Rex played the Chatham gig, with the set that was used throughout the tour, as follows:

20th Century Boy, Jeepster, Funky London Childhood, New York City, Solid Gold Easy Action, Children Of The Revolution, Telegram Sam, Debora*, Ride A White Swan*, Dreamy Lady*, London Boys, Teenage Dream, Hot Love and Get It On. (*part of an acoustic medley)

After Chatham, the band played St Albans and Folkestone. Then it was on to Southend, where, during the acoustic set, the audience began to sing 'Life's A Gas'; Marc sang along with them — and thereafter, not only did Marc add 'Life's A Gas' to the set, but also slotted in 'One Inch Rock' for good measure.

Marc waving to fans from coach after the gig at the Cliffs Pavilion, Southend on Sea, 8th February, 1976.

There was a three-day break before the next gig at The Floral Hall, Southport. Once again, during the acoustic set Marc took everyone by surprise, this time by playing a verse of 'Mambo Sun' (from the 'Electric Warrior' album) which he had never played live in concert before.

After the gig, Marc and the band went to the Clifton Hotel, Southport. Marc was quite talkative that evening and spoke at length to us and another group of fans that had managed to locate his whereabouts; he even sang 'Happy Birthday' to my friend, Phil Bowser, who was twenty-one that day.

Alf Bradley asked Marc if he would be including 'Jupiter Liar' (from the 'Futuristic Dragon' album) in the set, to which Marc replied 'Yes, we might do "Liar"', and then stood up and literally screamed out the first verse ... He also commented on the fact that 'All Alone' was his favourite track from the 'Futuristic Dragon' album.

Later on, someone handed Marc a copy of the 1969 Tyrannosaurus Rex tour programme, which contained the lyrics to 'Demon Queen'. Marc couldn't remember too much about the song, only that he recorded it in the late 60's with David Bowie

Marc chatting to fans in Southport, where he played the Floral Hall, 12th February, 1976.

Marc posing at the Clifton Hotel, Southport, 13th February, 1976.

(although Bowie now claims that he has never heard of the track). He also went on to talk about Gary Glitter, saying, 'Musically he's shit, but he's a good gardener — he grows nice tomatoes!'

In the morning, the whole of the T.Rex entourage made their way to the next gig, which was at Newark in Nottinghamshire, followed by a date at Withernsea, Humberside, on St Valentine's Day.

This show, at Withernsea Pavilion, was destined to be a failure. The promotion for the gig was virtually non-existent: the event had been billed as a 'St Valentine's Day

Dance', without a mention of T.Rex, and as a result the audience were mainly there for the disco and seemed uninterested in watching a live band. Halfway through the set, Marc finally had enough and shouted out, 'How do you expect me to play when you're walking around eating fucking hamburgers?'

Near the end of the show, a few fans got over-enthusiastic and invaded the stage; unfortunately in the process they pulled Marc over and made his guitar go out of tune. Marc threw his Gibson Les Paul angrily to the floor, stormed off stage and punched his fist through a glass panelled door, cutting himself badly enough to need stitches in his right wrist. A week later, he claimed in the newspapers that a fan had thrown a bottle of champagne through his dressing-room window, and that it was this that caused his injury.

Marc at home in Holmead Road, Chelsea, with wrist cut after the incident with the glass-panelled door at Withernsea . . .

Marc outside the Holiday Inn, Birmingham, on his way to BRMB Radio, 23rd February, 1976.

The night after the Withernsea disaster, T.Rex played in Sunderland, where Marc's repertoire included 'Conesuala' (from the 'Prophets, Seers and Sages' album). Halfway through the acoustic set, a fan jumped on stage and threw his arms around Marc's neck, causing him to choke so badly that he had to leave the stage. But he returned a few moments later, saying brightly, 'I almost swallowed my Adam's apple!'

A two-day break followed. The next stop for T.Rex was The Lyceum Ballroom in London, which was the first London gig they'd done since 1972, followed by the highlight of the tour, at Dunstable's Queensway Hall. Marc talked a lot to the crowd and sang segments of various songs, including Frankie Vaughan's 'Give Me The Moonlight' and Paul Simon's 'Fifty Ways To Leave Your Lover'. He also talked about how he had 'ripped off' 'Jeepster' from Howlin' Wolf's 'You'll Be Mine', before going on to sing a few lines from the song.

After Dunstable, T.Rex played Bournemouth and then had another two days off.

The next date was at the Town Hall in Birmingham. Marc arrived during the early afternoon and went to the local radio station, BRMB, to do an interview to promote the 'Futuristic Dragon' album. While on air he invited Roy Wood to go along to the gig at the Town Hall that evening; Roy did actually turn up, but declined a further invitation to come up on stage.

At this gig, the venue was completely sold out, to the extent that, due to public demand, seats *behind* the stage had to be sold (which meant that the dragon back-drop could not be used). After the show, Marc had to be escorted by the police, as hundreds of fans were blocking the entrance of the Holiday Inn where the band were staying. However, he managed to get out later that evening, and went to Barbarella's night club with Roy Wood, in order to see The Fatback Band play.

From Birmingham, T.Rex had to travel to Manchester for the next show, which was at the Free Trade Hall. After the gig, Marc was unlucky enough to be attacked by a wayward David Bowie fan, who punched him in the face, knocking him out and

Marc with bruised eye after the incident with the Bowie fan . . .

Marc at the Albany Hotel, Glasgow, March, 1976.

shouting, 'Bowie's much better than you!' Marc's chief roadie, Mick O'Halloran, gave chase, but the Bowie fan managed to make a quick getaway.

T.Rex rested for two days before playing their next gig, this time at the Floral Pavilion, New Brighton, Merseyside. When Marc arrived, he was wearing a crash helmet, which hid a badly bruised eye . . .!

The next day, Marc and the band went up to Scotland; once there, Marc and Gloria booked into the Albany Hotel, while the band stayed at the Pond – both in Glasgow, as the first Scottish show was at the Glasgow Apollo (a gig notable for the fact that Marc started to recite prose in the middle of 'Get It On'). Dates followed at Falkirk and Motherwell, where Marc had, by this time, added the old Marty Wilde hit, 'Teenager In Love' to his acoustic set. At one point on their way to Motherwell, Marc and his old friend, Jeff Dexter, stopped the tour coach so that they could use

Tour Dates		
5	February	Central Hall, Chatham
6	February	City Hall, St Albans
7	February	Leas Cliffe Hall, Folkestone
8	February	Cliffs Pavilion, Southend
12	February	Floral Hall, Southport
13	February	Palace Theatre, Newark
14	February	Grand Pavilion, Withernsea
15	February	Empire Theatre, Sunderland
18	February	Lyceum Ballroom, London
19	February	Queensway Hall, Dunstable
20	February	Winter Gardens, Bournemouth
23	February	Town Hall, Birmingham
24	February	Free Trade Hall, Manchester
28	February	Floral Hall Pavilion, New Brighton
1	March	Apollo, Glasgow
3	February	Municipal Hall, Falkirk
4	February	Concert Hall, Motherwell
6	February	Grand Hall, Kilmarnock

the public toilets in Glasgow. When they came out, they were both laughing. Marc popped his head through the window of our car (we were following the coach) and said, 'We're just talking about Syd Barrett's cock' — and then burst out laughing. Perhaps as some kind of karmic revenge, Marc went down with the flu during the gig that night and, in turn, had to cut the show short, omitting four songs from the set. The final gig, which should have taken place at Kilmarnock on 6th March, had to be cancelled too.

Sadly, Marc was drinking heavily right from the beginning of the tour, and was drunk during every performance, inevitably forgetting the lyrics of his most memorable songs. In defence of the tour however, it should be said that Marc pleased many of his fans, as he made the shows something of a T.Rex 'family' occasion, talking to individual members of the audience, playing requests and also singing some of the songs that he himself had been influenced by.

Marc opening a present from a fan, on the tour coach after Gloria's gig supporting Bob Marley at Belle Vue, Manchester, 27th June, 1976. Gloria was Marley's support for the whole tour, and played the following venues: Hammersmith Odeon, London*; Cardiff Castle*; Odeon, Birmingham*; Colston Hall, Bristol; Exeter University; Leeds University; Belle Vue, Manchester*. Marc attended the starred gigs.

T.REX IN FRANCE

In February, 1977, T.Rex played a short, low-key tour of France. This was intended to be a warm-up for the British tour in March of that year, although a lot of the dates were cancelled: however, the last two, in Paris and Troarn, did go ahead. In Paris, all the main streets had giant posters of Marc plastered on the walls; these were simply pictures of Marc with the words 'T.Rex' across the top. The effect was very striking. The band was booked to play a hall called Le Bataclan in Paris, but, for some reason, the venue was changed at the last minute to Le Nashville, a very exclusive and expensive nightclub, which was full to capacity with a mixture of people, including a small gathering of T.Rex fans.

The band came on stage at 1.30 a.m. and got underway with a powerful version of 'Jeepster'. Then it was full speed ahead through 'Visions Of Domino' (new lyrics set to the backing track of 'Funky London Childhood'), 'New York City' and a new song, 'Groove A Little'. Then came an up-tempo version of 'The Soul Of My Suit' (a song first featured on the 1975 tour), 'I Love To Boogie', another new song, called 'Hang Ups', the old favourite, 'Hot Love' and finally, for the encore, 'Get It On'.

Promotional poster for the 1977 T. Rex tour of France.

Marc was certainly starting off 1977 in the right direction, with a new sound from a new band. He seemed so agile and eager; and with Miller Anderson backing him up, he had the freedom to display his guitar playing as well. For the first time in years Marc was playing several songs from a new album. He had dropped both the acoustic set from the 1976 tour and some of the old songs like '20th Century Boy' and 'Teenage Dream'. Even better, he was obviously very pleased with the reaction he was getting: the audience was really enthusiastic and there was an extremely good atmosphere in the club.

After the gig, Marc said that he was really happy with the new band — Dino Dines (keyboards), Miller Anderson (guitar), Herbie Flowers (bass) and Tony Newman (drums). He said they were playing better each time they gigged and that they were the best rock 'n' roll band in the world. He also mentioned that he was looking forward to the British tour and that he intended to record two gigs, one at London's Rainbow Theatre and one possible other, for inclusion on a live album to be released in the future.

T. Rex in concert at Le Nashville, Paris, 11th February, 1977. *From left to right:* Miller, Marc and Herbie.

The last French gig, on 12th February, 1977, was in a small village called Troarn, just outside Caen, at a sports hall called La Salle Des Fêtes. Once inside the hall, there was a worry that the gig might have to be cancelled, as fluctuations in the electricity supply meant there was a danger of equipment blowing up ... However, after much discussion, it was decided that the gig would go ahead as planned.

T.Rex came on stage at midnight, and played a set that was basically the same as the previous nights, although after 'Hot Love' Marc took everyone by surprise by playing another new song, 'Dandy In The Underworld', the title track of the forthcoming album. It sounded great and it seemed obvious that this was going to be one of Marc's classic tracks. The audience reaction was a bit subdued at first, but by the end they were just as enthusiastic as the previous night's crowd.

Throughout both gigs, Marc was using both his Fender Stratocaster and his new, cherry-red Gibson Les Paul; he had said the previous day that he had been very upset when his vintage Les Paul was stolen earlier in the year.

Dino, Miller, Herbie and Tony on the ferry from Dieppe to Dover, returning from their tour of France, 13th February, 1977.

For tour ads

$2\frac{1}{2}$ by $2\frac{1}{2}$

T.REX ~~~~
gig
tours

R.M
mm
nME

March 1st

every page

for album -

~~~~~~~~~~

whos a
DANDY in
the underworld

week
before
page ads

THE DANDY IN THE UNDERWORLD TOUR — 1977

After extensive rehearsals at the Alaska Studios, underneath the arches in Waterloo, T.Rex began their nine-date tour of the UK, commencing in Newcastle on 10th March, 1977.

On the eve of the tour, EMI Records held a party at The Roxy (a London club which had been opened in 1977, specifically as a place where new wave and punk bands could play) celebrating the release of the new album, 'Dandy In The Underworld'. Among the guests invited were Donovan, Harry Nilsson, Lionel Bart, Sid Vicious, Johnny Rotten, Billy Idol, Mike Mansfield, Rockpile and members of The Vibrators and The Damned. The latter had been personally chosen by Marc to support T.Rex throughout the 'Dandy' tour after he had seen them perform live. Marc once said, 'I chose The Damned to support us because one of them had the good sense to wear a Marc Bolan T-shirt.'

The opening night of the tour at the Newcastle City Hall was the first in what would be a string of sell-out dates. T.Rex used the same set-list for the whole of the tour, kicking off with 'Jeepster', followed by 'Visions Of Domino', 'New York City', 'The Soul Of My Suit', 'Groove A Little', 'Telegram Sam', 'Hang Ups', 'Debora', 'I Love To Boogie', 'Teen Riot Structure', 'Dandy', 'Hot Love' and 'Get It On'. Although the official release date for the album was 11 March, two thousand copies had been brought along and were on sale in the foyer after the show. They sold out in twenty minutes . . .

Shortly after the gig, a party was held for the band, friends and press at the Newcastle Holiday Inn, where champagne flowed until the early hours of the morning.

After the second date, in Manchester, T.Rex drove to Glasgow for their gig at the Apollo on 12th March. However, the show had to be postponed for one night, as the roadies had left vital electrical leads at the previous night's venue; as a result, the gig originally planned for 13th March, at Hanley, Stoke-on-Trent, had to be cancelled indefinitely.

From Glasgow the band drove by coach to the next gig in Bristol and then on to Birmingham, where a few of Marc's old friends attended the gig: Steve Harley, Steve

Left: Marc's notes and ideas for music press advertisements for the forthcoming 'Dandy in the Underworld' tour and album, 1977.

Gibbons and Robert Plant, all of whom went backstage later.

After the Birmingham show, there was a two-day break before the next gig at the Rainbow in London, where once again some of Marc's celebrity friends turned up for the show: Billy Idol, John Miles, Gary Holton (of The Heavy Metal Kids and star of the 80's TV series, *Auf Wiedersehen, Pet*) and Alvin Stardust.

From London, T.Rex made their way to West Runton for their gig at the Pavilion, where members of the band's families attended the show. Afterwards, the band were driven back to London, where Marc was dropped off at Victoria and caught a taxi home.

The next morning, the tour coach went to Portsmouth for the final date of the 'Dandy' tour, at the Locarno, where Marc invited The Damned on stage for the *grand finale*, playing 'Get It On'. After the gig, the band were again driven back to London. The tour coach dropped Marc off at Putney Bridge at about two in the morning; he promptly telephoned his dad and asked him to come and pick him up and take him home!

T. Rex at the Colston Hall, Bristol, on 14th March, 1977. In the background are Herbie Flowers, Mick O'Halloran (Marc's personal roadie) and Captain Sensible of The Damned.

Top: Marc buying magazines at a service station on the M6 motorway, after the concert at the Birmingham Odeon on 17th March, 1977.

Bottom: Captain Sensible and Marc playing 'Get It On' at the Portsmouth Locarno on the 20th March, 1977.

In general, although the 'Dandy' tour was not in the same league as events such as the 'Futuristic Dragon' tour of 1976, it was a great success. The band were very well rehearsed and together, while the sound quality was probably the finest of Marc's career: a sure sign that Marc was well on his way back to super-stardom . . .

Tour Dates

10 March	City Hall, Newcastle
11 March	Apollo, Manchester
12 March	Apollo, Glasgow
13 March	Victoria Hall, Hanley
14 March	Colston Hall, Bristol
17 March	Odeon Theatre, Birmingham
18 March	Rainbow Theatre, London
19 March	Pavilion, West Runton
20 March	Locarno, Portsmouth

T. Rex at the Gröna Lund, a large fairground in the heart of Stockholm, Sweden, on 24th May, 1977. That was a one-off event, not considered to be part of the 'Dandy in the Underworld' tour, and it proved to be T. Rex's last gig.

6. IT'S COSMIC ROCK! — THE ESSENTIAL SINGLES AND ALBUMS, 1965–77

The following section contains a personal selection of what we consider to be the essential singles and albums released in Marc's lifetime. We did not think it necessary to include a *complete* discography for several reasons, not least of which is that the task has already been attempted in several other books; the biographies *Born To Boogie* by Chris Welch and Simon Napier-Bell, and *Electric Warrior* by Paul Sinclair both contain versions, although probably the best and most comprehensive is the *Marc Bolan Discography*, compiled by the Marc Bolan fan club and published by Omnibus. Also, a *truly* complete discography would be virtually impossible to compile, because Marc's career was never documented as well as the likes of The Beatles, Presley, Hendrix *et al.*, and copies of various releases crop up from the most unlikely countries and places. We decided therefore to include only the most important British releases, as we felt that they are the prime source for collectors and fans.

To add a little colour to this chapter, we have incorporated various snippets of information which you may find of interest, along with some of Marc's jottings, photos and manuscripts, to whet your appetite!

Idea for a song?

Essential Singles

THE WIZARD/BEYOND THE RISING SUN

Released: 19th November, 1965 (Decca Records)

Producer: Jim Economides

This represented Marc's grand entrance into the world of pop music. The lyrics on the track loosely refer to his weekend meeting with his 'wizard friend' in Paris.

Highest chart position: Non-entry

THE THIRD DEGREE/SAN FRANCISCO POET

Released: 3rd June, 1966 (Decca Records)

Producer: Jim Economides

Marc was never happy with this recording, as he felt it remained incomplete. The B-side, 'San Francisco Poet', was based on one of Marc's early favourite songs, 'San Francisco Bay Blues', by the old bluesman, Jesse Fuller.

Highest chart position: Non-entry

HIPPY GUMBO/MISFIT

Released: 25th November, 1966 (Parlophone/Columbia Records)

Producer: Simon Napier-Bell

Highest chart position: Non-entry

DESDEMONA/REMEMBER THOMAS À BECKETT (Available in PS)

Released: 24th May, 1967 (Track Records)

Producer: Simon Napier-Bell

'Desdemona' was a Bolan composition for John's Children that bubbled under the charts for a while. At the time, the picture sleeve caused some controversy, as it featured a photo of a woman superimposed over the band, who was expressing sexual pleasure. This was the only record, out of all those that Marc would be associated with, that ever caused the BBC to initiate a ban.

Highest chart position: Non-entry

MIDSUMMER NIGHT'S SCENE/SARA CRAZY CHILD

Released: Withdrawn before distribution date, June/July 1967 (Track Records)

Producer: Simon Napier-Bell

A very small number of copies of this, both sides of which were Bolan compositions, did manage to reach fans, as the band sold copies at the John's Children club in Leatherhead, Surrey. John's Children would continue to record Bolan compositions even after Marc had left the band.

Highest chart position: N/a

DEBORA/CHILD STAR (Demo-PS)

Released: 19th April, 1968 (Regal Zonophone [Blue-Label])

Producer: Tony Visconti

Tyrannosaurus Rex was born!

Highest chart position: No. 34

ONE INCH ROCK/SALAMANDA PALAGANDA (Demo-PS)

Released: 23rd August, 1968 (Regal Zonophone [Blue Label])

Producer: Tony Visconti

Marc released two versions of 'One Inch Rock': one was this release, while the other was the electric version included on the 'T.Rex' album of two years later. (This does not include the take used on the 'Doves' album.)

Highest chart position: No. 28

PEWTER SUITOR/WARLORD OF THE ROYAL CROCODILES

Released: 14th January, 1969 (Regal Zonophone [Red Label])

Producer: Tony Visconti

'Pewter Suitor' was never made available on album in Marc's lifetime.

Highest chart position: Non-entry

KING OF THE RUMBLING SPIRES/DO YOU REMEMBER? (Demo-PS)
Released: 25th July, 1969 (Regal Zonophone [Red Label])
Producer: Tony Visconti

This was the first Tyrannosaurus Rex single to feature an electric guitar, but also Steve Took's last single with Marc.

Highest chart position: No. 44

BY THE LIGHT OF A MAGICAL MOON/FIND A LITTLE WOOD
Released: 20th January, 1970 (Regal Zonophone [Red Label])
Producer: Tony Visconti

The last single made under the name Tyrannosaurus Rex.

Highest chart position: Non-entry

OH BABY/UNIVERSAL LOVE
Released: August, 1970 (Bell Records)
Producer: Tony Visconti

Marc wrote 'Oh Baby', but released it under the pseudonym 'Dib Cochran and The Earwigs'. Tony Visconti sang lead vocals, while the rest of the band was as follows: Marc Bolan (guitar/BV's), Mickey Finn (percussion) and, disputedly, Rick Wakeman (piano) and David Bowie (BV's). Although not a T.Rex record, it remains, nevertheless, of great interest to Marc Bolan fans.

Highest chart position: Non-entry

RIDE A WHITE SWAN/IS IT LOVE/SUMMERTIME BLUES (PS)
Released: 2nd October, 1970 (Fly Records)*
Producer: Tony Visconti

*Before Fly Records became permanently established, some singles did leak out on the old Regal Zonophone label, as well as on the Octopus label before it transformed into Fly.

This was the first single under the abbreviated name T.Rex; due to Marc's value-for-money policy, the B-side on this as well as many other T.Rex records had two or more tracks.

Highest chart position: No. 2

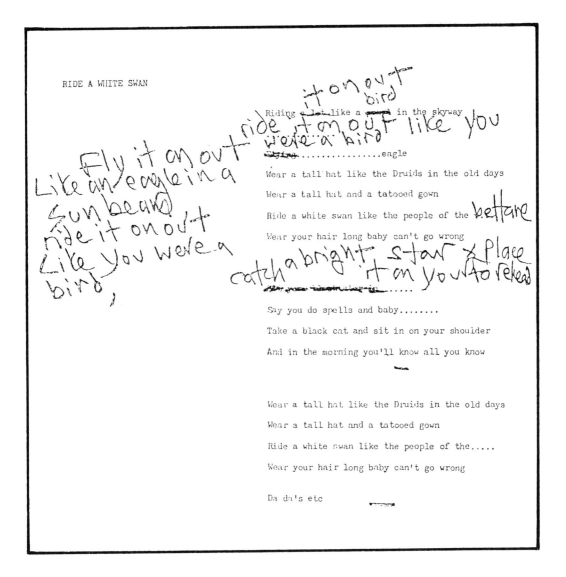

Lyrics to 'Ride a White Swan' typed out by June, with handwritten additions and amendments by Marc. The single would stay in the Top Fifty for a total of twenty weeks.

HOT LOVE/WOODLAND ROCK/THE KING OF THE MOUNTAIN COMETH
Released: 19th February, 1971 (Fly Records)
Producer: Tony Visconti

This was T.Rex's first No. 1. The original acetate had instructions for an alternative fadeout at just over two minutes; however, the final cut ran to a little under five minutes.

Highest chart position: No. 1

GET IT ON/THERE WAS A TIME/RAW RAMP/ELECTRIC BOOGIE (PS)
Released: 2nd July, 1971 (Fly Records)
Producer: Tony Visconti

Highest chart position: No. 1. Reached No. 1 in U.S.A. too.

JEEPSTER/LIFE'S A GAS
Released: 1st November, 1971 (Fly Records)
Producer: Tony Visconti

Marc freely admitted that 'Jeepster' was his remake of 'You'll Be Mine' by the old blues singer, Howlin' Wolf.

Highest chart position: No. 2

TELEGRAM SAM/CADILAC/BABY STRANGE
Released: 21st January, 1972 (EMI-T.Rex Wax Co.)
Producer: Tony Visconti

Marc's own record label was born with the release of what would be the first in a line of special T.Rex red and blue sleeves and labels. The 'hidden treasure' track, 'Cadilac' (*sic*), was not released on album during Marc's lifetime.

Highest chart position: No. 1

DEBORA/ONE INCH ROCK/THE WOODLAND BOP/THE SEAL OF SEASONS (PS)
Released: 24th March, 1972 (Magni-Fly)
Producer: Tony Visconti

'Debora' and 'One Inch Rock' were originally released as singles in 1968. 'The Woodland Bop' was taken from the 'Beard of Stars' album, while 'The Seal Of Seasons' was taken from the 'Unicorn' LP. Fly reissued this EP at the height of Marc's career.

Highest chart position: No. 7

Marc performing 'Hot Love' on *Top of the Pops* (1971). It stayed at No. 1 for six weeks, and spent a total of seventeen weeks in the Top 50.

METAL GURU/THUNDERWING/LADY
Released: 5th May, 1972 (EMI-T.Rex Wax Co.)
Producer: Tony Visconti

This was the last single T.Rex produced that topped the charts. Marc used to say that he sometimes wished for a place where he could go for a little peace and quiet, a place 'without telephones'; he felt that such an existence would be similar to that of a god. It seems that the Metal Guru is this god, 'all alone without a telephone'.

Highest chart position: No. 1

CHILDREN OF THE REVOLUTION/JITTERBUG LOVE/SUNKEN RAGS
Released: 8th September, 1972 (EMI-T.Rex Wax Co.)
Producer: Tony Visconti

'Children' was issued with a red and white T.Rex sleeve and label, as opposed to the traditional red and blue; the track was intended to be a taster for the forthcoming T.Rex feature film, *Born To Boogie*. 'Sunken Rags' was originally recorded acoustically and donated to the 1972 charity triple album, 'Glastonbury Fayre'.

Highest chart position: No. 2

SOLID GOLD EASY ACTION/BORN TO BOOGIE.
Released: 1st December, 1972 (EMI-T.Rex Wax Co.)
Producer: Tony Visconti

Before the intro on 'Born To Boogie', Marc recites a Christmas message which, to date, has not been included on any album.

Highest chart position: No. 2

XMAS T.REX FLEXI-DISC
Released: December, 1972
Producer: Tony Visconti/Marc Bolan

This was sent out to all members of the T.Rex fan club. Based on the early Beatles fan club flexi-discs of the 60's, it featured Marc, Mickey Finn and Steve Currie; Bill

memo - grover

ads in melody maker
nme.

week of release London - friday ⎱
                                   ⎰ '83
week later Yorkshire - Saturday ⎱
                          Saturday

interviews in   mm
                 nme
                 record mirror
                 fan
                 Music star
                 Disc
            2 nationals

ring attham film goinggood
      altert   anya
re grover + big Carrott
              — pto

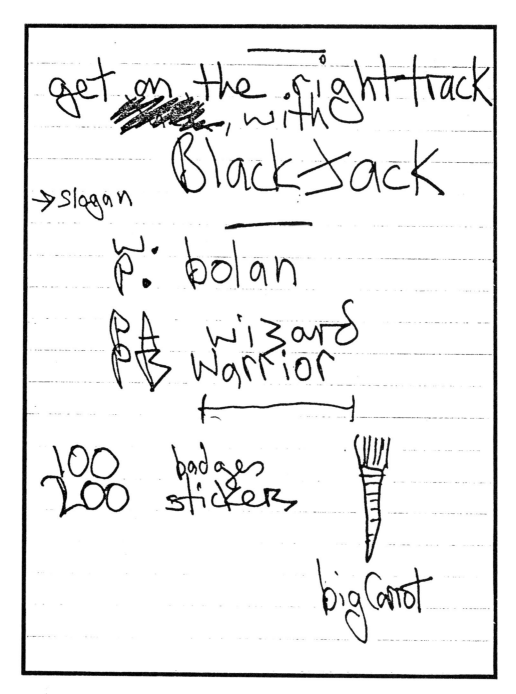

get on the right track with Black Jack

→ slogan

P. bolan

wizard warrior

100
200

badges
stickers

big Carrot

Previous page and above: Extracts from Marc's notebook with promotional ideas for 'The Groover' and 'Blackjack'. 'Film going good' refers to *Born to Boogie*. The badges and stickers mentioned above never actually materialized.

Legend was not around for the recording, so a female voice was substituted! The flexi included spoken messages from the band, interspersed with various ad-libbed songs and a backward guitar solo from 'Ballrooms Of Mars'.

Highest chart position: N/a

20TH CENTURY BOY/FREE ANGEL
Released: 2nd March, 1973 (EMI-T.Rex Wax Co.)
Producer: Tony Visconti (but, debatably, Marc Bolan)

For the backing vocals on '20th Century Boy', Marc employed the talents of Vicky Brown (Joe Brown's wife and Sam Brown's mother), Sue and Sunny (from the original 60's line-up of Brotherhood Of Man), and the famous session singer, Barry St John (who has recorded with, amongst others, Pink Floyd and Rod Stewart).

Highest chart position: No. 3

THE GROOVER/MIDNIGHT
Released: 1st June, 1973 (EMI-T.Rex Wax Co.)
Producer: Tony Visconti/Marc Bolan

Some of Marc's finest guitar work features on the flip side, 'Midnight', a rough/working version of which can be found on the 'Rarities Two' album (a 1991 fan club release).

Highest chart position: No. 4

BLACKJACK/SQUINT EYE MANGLE
Released: 10th August, 1973 (EMI records)
Producer: Marc Bolan

This single was issued under the pseudonym, 'Big Carrot'. Both tracks were written by Marc and, at best, sound like a T.Rex backing track. The vocals were by Gloria Jones, Pat Hall and Stephanie Spruill.

Highest chart position: Non-entry

TRUCK ON (TYKE)/SITTING HERE
Released: 16th November, 1973 (EMI-T.Rex Wax Co.)
Producer: Tony Visconti

Gloria Jones made her T.Rex début here, singing BV's. Marc's pronunciation of the word 'dinosaurs' was inspired by the Hollywood Argyles' 1960 hit, 'Alley Oop'. The only time T.Rex performed 'Truck On' on television was on Granada TV's *Lift Off*, as Bill Legend had already left by that time, Mickey Finn stood in on drums.

Highest chart position: No. 12

TEENAGE DREAM/SATISFACTION PONY
Released: 28th January, 1974 (EMI-T.Rex Wax Co.)
Producer: Tony Visconti/Marc Bolan

This was the first single credited to 'Marc Bolan and T.Rex'. The A-side, 'Teenage Dream', was considered anthemic and in a similar vein to Dylan's 'Like A Rolling Stone', while the B-side, 'Satisfaction Pony', was not released on album in Marc's lifetime. However, a superior mix can be found on the 'Rarities Two' LP (*ibid*).

Highest chart position: No. 13

JASPER C. DEBUSSY/HIPPY GUMBO/THE PERFUMED GARDEN OF GULLIVER SMITH (PS)
Released: 19th June, 1974 (Track Records)
Producer: Simon Napier-Bell

All the above tracks were written by Marc in 1966 while he was managed by Napier-Bell. 'Jasper' and 'Hippy Gumbo' were tasters from the 'Beginning Of Doves' LP. 'The Perfumed Garden', based on the Chalice Garden in Glastonbury, was never released in any other format during Marc's lifetime.

Highest chart position: Non-entry

LIGHT OF LOVE/EXPLOSIVE MOUTH
Released: 5th July, 1974 (EMI-T.Rex Wax Co.)
Producer: Marc Bolan

The official follow-up to 'Teenage Dream' was the first single since 'Ride A White Swan' not to reach the Top Twenty.

Highest chart position: No. 22

Photo of Marc from the 'Light of Love' sessions, taken while waiting for a video shoot, 1974.

ZIP GUN BOOGIE/SPACE BOSS
Released: 1st November, 1974 (EMI-T.Rex Wax Co.)
Producer: Marc Bolan

This was the first single credited to 'Marc Bolan' alone, without T.Rex, and is probably the most uninspiring Bolan A-side composition on record.

Highest chart position: No. 41

NEW YORK CITY/CHROME SITAR
Released: 27th June, 1975 (EMI-T.Rex Wax Co.)
Producer: Marc Bolan

Highest chart position: No. 15

DREAMY LADY/DO YOU WANNA DANCE/DOCK OF THE BAY
Released: 26th September, 1975 (EMI-T.Rex Wax Co.)
Producer: Marc Bolan

Known as the 'T.Rex Disco Party', this included the first cover versions on a T.Rex single since the 1970 release, 'Summertime Blues'. Gloria Jones sang lead vocals on 'Dock Of The Bay' (written by Otis Redding) and Marc sang the old Bobby Freeman classic, 'Do You Wanna Dance' (though it was Cliff Richard who had the hit in the UK with his cover version).

A promotional video was shot for 'Dreamy Lady' which featured Marc in a silver suit, lying on a revolving podium. The only known screening was on the children's TV show, *Tiswas.*

Highest chart position: No. 30

MARC'S XMAS BOX: CHRISTMAS BOP/TELEGRAM SAM/METAL GURU
Released: Planned release date, 1st December, 1975
Producer: Marc Bolan

Records were never pressed, although labels had been printed and a catalogue number issued: MARC 12 on EMI-T.Rex Wax Co. 'Christmas Bop' eventually saw release in 1982, while another song, 'Reelin' An' A Rockin' An' A Bopping' An' A

Bolan', recorded during the Christmas Bop sessions at the Scorpio Studios, London, can be found on the 'Rarities Three' album (a 1991 fan club issue).

Highest chart position: N/a

LONDON BOYS/SOLID BABY
Released: 20th February, 1976 (EMI-T.Rex Wax Co.)
Producer: Marc Bolan

Highest chart position: No. 40

I LOVE TO BOOGIE/BABY BOOMERANG
Released: 5th June, 1976 (EMI-T.Rex Wax Co.)
Producer: Marc Bolan

Marc's roadie, Micky Marmalade (a name chosen by Marc, as Micky had formerly been a roadie for the group of the same name) recalls that 'I Love To Boogie' was

Marc at the opening of Glasgow airport, June 1976, where he was interviewed by Radio Clyde to promote 'I Love to Boogie'.

written by Marc while living in Monte Carlo in 1975. Originally recorded for demo purposes only, Marc thought it had a great 'feel', so decided to release it as it stood, even leaving the hi-hat count in for good measure. 'Boogie' was a real return to form, even though it was a blatant rip-off of Webb Pierce's 1956 composition, 'Teenage Boogie'.

It is worthy of note that 'I Love To Boogie' was the only twelve-inch single released in Marc's lifetime; this version was only available in France, with a leopardskin-print sleeve and a label that stated 'Special Disco Mix'.

Highest chart position: No. 13

LASER LOVE/LIFE'S AN ELEVATOR
Released: 17th September, 1976 (EMI-T.Rex Wax Co.)
Producer: Marc Bolan

A small quantity of official badges were made to promote this single, featuring a photo of Marc in his 'Bolantino' phase, with the wording 'A new age of Bolan — T.Rex Unchained'; however, despite this promotion and the fact that 'Laser Love' was a potential hit, the production was weak and the single never entered the Top Thirty.

The flip side was, however, superb. It featured some beautiful acoustic guitar playing by both Marc and Miller Anderson (previously of Keef Hartley and Savoy Brown).

Highest chart position: No. 41

TO KNOW HIM IS TO LOVE HIM/CITY PORT
Released: 14th January, 1977 (EMI Records)
Producer: Marc Bolan

This was not a T.Rex record, but a Marc Bolan and Gloria Jones record. Marc changed the lyrics of this 1958 song (originally performed by The Teddy Bears and written by Phil Spector) to the more appropriate 'To Know *You* Is To Love You'.

'City Port' is an essential classic, sadly tucked away on the B-side.

Highest chart position: Non-entry

Marc's handwritten lyrics to the T. Rex single, 'Laser Love'.

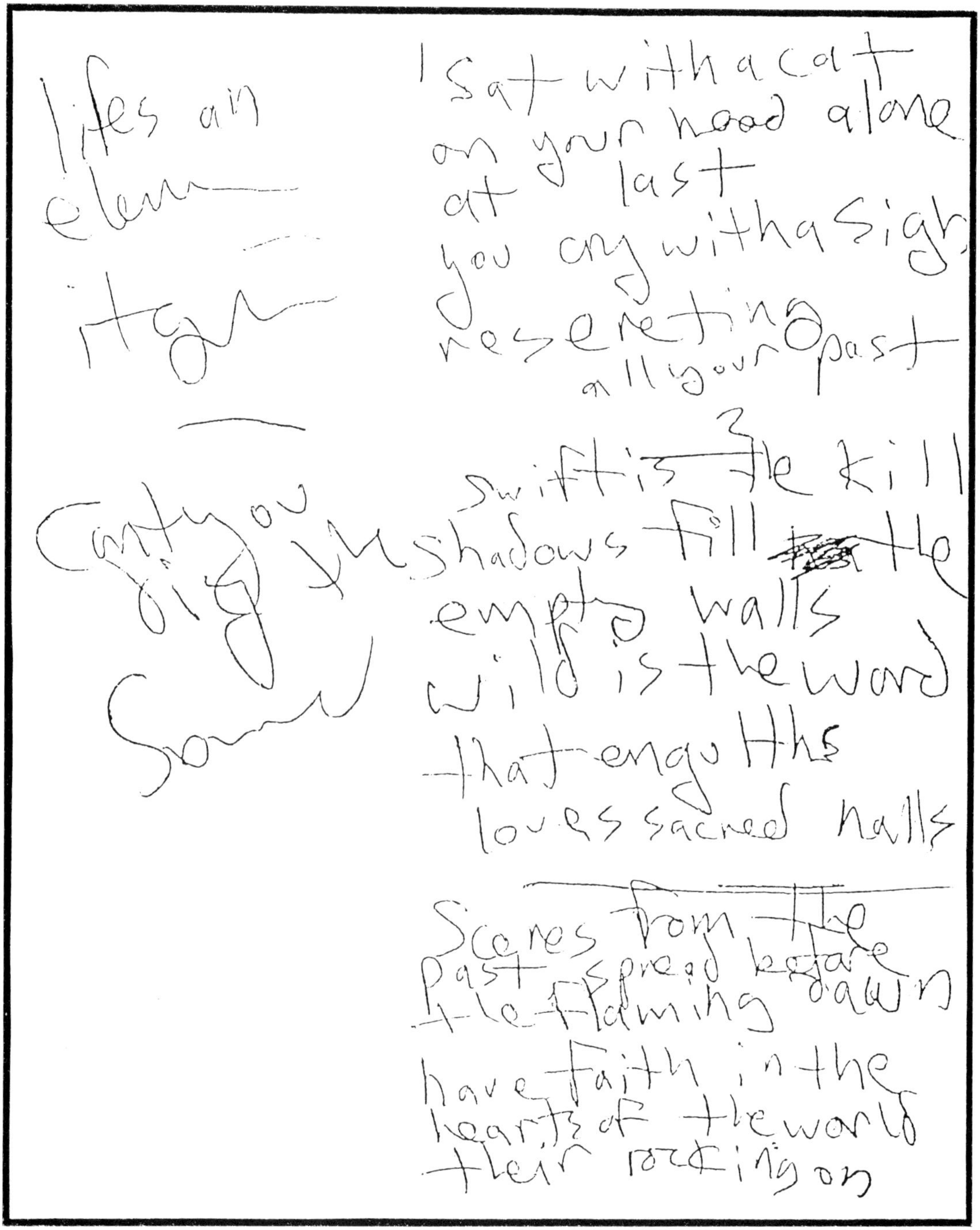

lifes an
eleva
itar

I sat with a cat
on your head alone
at last
you cry with a sigh
reserecting
all your past

Cant you
dig it
Soul

swift is the kill
shadows fill the
empty walls
wild is the word
that engulfths
loves sacred halls

Scenes from the
past spread before
the flaming dawn
have faith in the
hearts of the world
their rocking on

Marc's handwritten lyrics to 'Life's an Elevator', the B-side to 'Laser Love'.

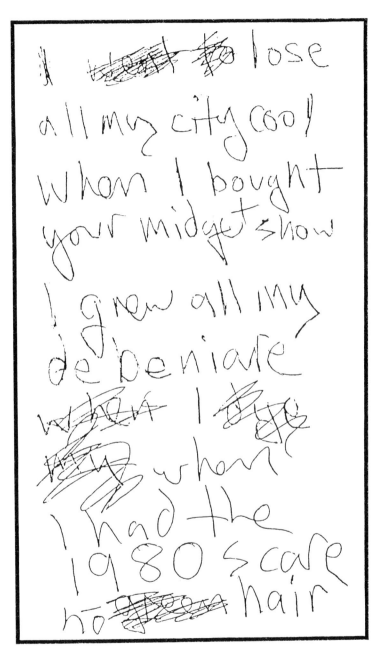

Original manuscript lyrics to 'City Port'. Although Marc had originally written 'green hair', to keep in with the current punk rock trend, he finally decided on 'no hair' (perhaps because of a fear of going bald?).

THE SOUL OF MY SUIT/ALL ALONE
Released: 12th March, 1977 (EMI-T.Rex Wax Co.)
Producer: Marc Bolan

A promotional video was made for this single, filmed on its date of release and featuring Marc in the 'Hall Of Mirrors' in Belle Vue, Manchester. This was a solo performance, with Marc posing with his guitar in the reflections of various different 'fat' and 'thin' mirrors.

Once, during a Capital Radio interview, Marc said that 'The Soul Of My Suit' was about a woman who hurt his ego.

Highest chart position: No. 42

DANDY IN THE UNDERWORLD/GROOVE A LITTLE/TAME MY TIGER (PS)
Released: 30th May, 1977 (EMI-T.Rex Wax Co.)
Producer: Marc Bolan

'Dandy' was a re-recorded version of the album track, with a change of lyrics from the word 'cocaine' to 'T.Rex'; the vocal sound on this version was noticeably nasal, as Marc had a cold at the time of recording.

This was the first official release since 'Get It On' in 1971 that incorporated a picture sleeve.

Highest chart position: Non-entry

CELEBRATE SUMMER/RIDE MY WHEELS (PS)
Released: 5th August, 1977 (EMI-T.Rex Wax Co.)
Producer: Marc Bolan

A good single that could have charted had it been promoted better, this was Marc's last single release before his death. Ironically enough, it contains the lyric, 'Summer is heaven in '77'.

Highest chart position: Non-entry

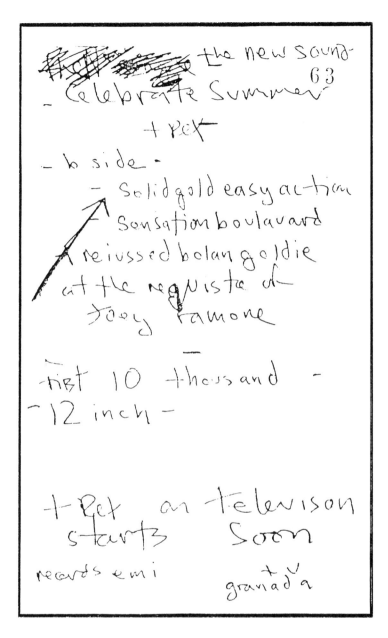

Handwritten notes for the single, 'Celebrate Summer'. It can be seen from these that Marc obviously had plans to release the single as a twelve-inch limited edition, featuring 'Solid Gold, Easy Action' and 'Sensation Boulevard' on the B-side. However, when the single was released, it was only available in seven-inch format with a picture sleeve and featured 'Ride My Wheels' on the flip side.

BOLAN'S BEST + ONE:RIDE A WHITE SWAN/THE MOTIVATOR/
JEEPSTER/DEMON QUEEN (PS)
Released: 5th August, 1977 (Cube Records)
Producer: Tony Visconti

The first three tracks on this EP were of no great interest to fans. However, 'Demon Queen', an outtake from the 1970 album 'A Beard Of Stars', definitely gave them the incentive to buy the record. Marc once stated in an interview that David Bowie played auto-harp on 'Demon Queen', but this is suspect.

Highest chart position: Non-entry

Essential Albums

MY PEOPLE WERE FAIR AND HAD SKY IN THEIR HAIR, BUT NOW THEY'RE
CONTENT TO WEAR STARS ON THEIR BROWS
Released: 7th July, 1968 (Regal Zonophone [Red Label])
Producer: Tony Visconti

'My People' was originally issued in both mono and stereo formats and included a lyric sheet; the début album by Tyrannosaurus Rex, it has, to date, the official longest title of a British LP, containing a staggering twenty words!

Marc dedicated the album to Aslan and the Old Narnians (characters from the C. S. Lewis novels about the mythical land of Narnia); Aslan was a God-like lion, which Marc thought was 'kinda nice'.

On the back sleeve, top centre, is the mythological 'Cornucopia' or 'Horn Of Plenty'. It is said that whoever possessed this artefact would get, in abundance, everything he or she desired.

Highest chart position: No. 15

PROPHETS, SEERS AND SAGES, THE ANGELS OF THE AGES
Released: 14th October, 1968 (Regal Zonophone [Red Label])
Producer: Tony Visconti

*Many tracks for this album were in fact written in 1969.

Woodcut by Gustave Doré (French illustrator, 1832-83) showing a scene from Dante's *Purgatorio* from the edition published in the UK in 1868. Marc used the illustrations for the sleeve design of his first album, 'My People Were Fair . . .'. This particular illustration was adapted for use in the lower half of the sleeve, which was executed by artist/designer George Underwood.

Another woodcut from Gustave Doré's edition of Dante, this one showing Milos, the infernal judge, sitting at the entrance to the Second Circle of Hell, in the *Inferno*. Part of this was also used for the sleeve design of 'My People Were Fair . . .', appearing in the bottom right-hand corner of the album's front cover.

'Prophets' was originally issued in both mono and stereo formats and contained a lyric sheet. The back sleeve featured a photograph (by Pete Sanders) of a bronze statue of Pan and a dancing woman. In Greek mythology Pan was sometimes portrayed as a small child with musical pipes, or as half man, half goat.

Highest chart position: Non-entry

UNICORN
Released: 18th May, 1969 (Regal Zonophone [Blue Label])
Producer: Tony Visconti

This was Steve Took's final album with Marc.

'Unicorn' was originally issued in a gate-fold sleeve, with lyrics on the inner cover. The photograph on the back sleeve was taken at DJ John Peel's home. Marc and Steve are surrounded by books by, among others, the philosopher and mystic, Kahil Gibran and the eighteenth-century English poet, William Blake, as well as a book of Shakespeare's stories simplified for children and the book *Fairies*, by Edward L. Gardner (pub. 1945). This latter is one of several publications dealing with the infamous hoax perpetrated at the beginning of the century by two young girls. In 1917, Elsie Wright (aged thirteen) and her cousin Frances Griffiths (aged ten) took some photos that were, at the time, regarded as the first full evidence of the existence of fairies. Sir Arthur Conan Doyle visited the couple and studied the photos before declaring them to be genuine, even going so far as to have them published in *The Strand* magazine.

However, at the tail end of the 1970s Elsie and Frances, both now in their seventies, revealed to the renowned author Arthur C. Clarke on the ITV show, *Arthur C. Clarke's Mysterious World*, that all the photos were faked. They announced that, because someone as distinguished as Sir Arthur Conan Doyle had believed them, they had felt obliged not to reveal their secret.

The 'Love One Another' plaque (behind Marc and Steve) and the sewing machine were both the property of Steve Took.

Highest chart position: No. 12

A BEARD OF STARS
Released: 22nd March, 1970 (Regal Zonophone [Red Label])
Producer: Tony Visconti

Not only was this Mickey Finn's début, but also an all-important transition for Marc, as this was the first time that he used an electric guitar on a Tyrannosaurus Rex LP (it would also be the only such occasion, as this was the last album released under the name 'Tyrannosaurus Rex'). Highest chart position: No. 21

T.REX
Released: 11th December, 1970 (Fly Records)
Producer: Tony Visconti

This was the first album to appear under the abbreviated name of 'T.Rex'. The photograph on the front sleeve shows Marc with his vintage Gibson guitar, which would be stolen from the back of a T.Rex roadie's van in January, 1977. It was later spotted by Marc in a London guitar shop, but, despite investigations by the police, it could not be proved that he was the rightful owner, so the guitar was never returned to him.

This album not only featured ex-Turtles Howard Kaylan and Mark Volman on backing vocals (who were to become a strong force in the 'sound' of T.Rex), but also introduced a very young Roy Thomas Baker, who, only a few years later, gained mass exposure and success by becoming producer for the top rock act, Queen.

Highest chart position: No. 13

BEST OF T.REX
Released: 25th March, 1971 (Fly Records)
Producer: Tony Visconti

This was an important release as it contained two previously unreleased tracks: 'Once Upon The Seas Of Abyssinia' and 'Blessed Wild Apple Girl'.

The photograph on the back sleeve was mistakenly reversed, showing Marc with his guitar left-handed. The sleeve-design idea was later used for the 1982 Queen LP entitled 'Hot Space'.

Highest chart position: No. 21

ELECTRIC WARRIOR
Released: 17th September, 1971 (Fly Records)
Producer: Tony Visconti

'Warrior' was the first album to include T.Rex's most famous line-up of Marc, Mickey Finn, Steve Currie and Bill Legend; it was also the first album to include a free poster. This was a black and white photo of T.Rex in Marc's front room.

The album included the song 'Cosmic Dancer', inspired by Marc's fascination with reincarnation and the after-life. When Marc died, his parents wanted the line, 'He danced from the womb to the tomb' (based on lyrics from 'Cosmic Dancer') to be engraved on Marc's plaque in Golders Green Crematorium. However, the crematorium officials would not give their permission.

Highest chart position: No. 1

Marc's original handwritten notes for the song 'Cosmic Dancer', which appeared on the LP 'Electric Warrior'. This album reached No. 1 on two separate occasions, spending a total of eight weeks at the top of the chart and remaining in the Top Fifty for forty-four weeks.

BOLAN BOOGIE

Released: 5th May, 1972 (Fly Records)

Producer: Tony Visconti

Not including reissues, this was the last T.Rex LP to be released by Fly Records.

Throughout Marc's career, up to 1977, the only cover version ever to be released on an album was the Eddie Cochran classic, 'Summertime Blues', included on 'Bolan Boogie'.

Highest chart position: No. 1

THE SLIDER

Released: 23rd July, 1972 (EMI-T.Rex Wax Co.)

Producer: Tony Visconti

Since its original release, there has been some dispute as to the creditation of the cover-sleeve photo. Although the photo is credited, on the inner jacket, to Ringo Starr, Tony Visconti claimed in later interviews that it was in fact his work.

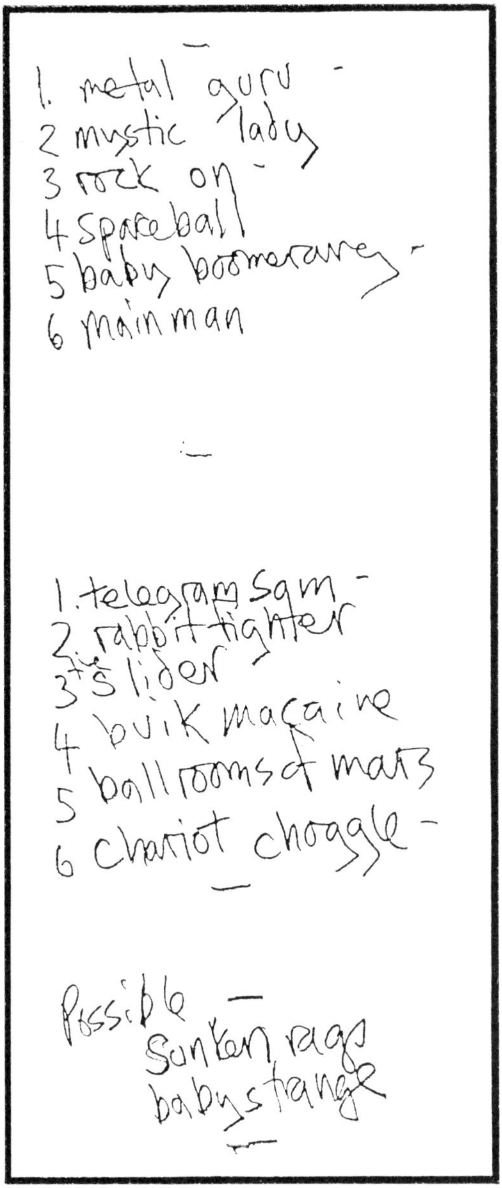

1. metal guru -
2 mystic lady
3 rock on -
4 spaceball
5 baby boomerang -
6 main man

1. telegram sam -
2. rabbit fighter
3 slider
4 buik macaine
5 ballrooms of mars
6 chariot choogle -

Possible -
   sunken rags
   baby strange

Left: Marc's rough design for the sleeve of 'The Slider', which spent eighteen weeks in the top 50. Although this idea for the back sleeve was shelved, it was later used as a working sheet for the follow-up album, 'Tanx'.

Above: Marc's original handwritten track listing for 'The Slider'.

One of Marc's original titles for the album was 'Rabbit Fighter', but he settled for 'The Slider' as he felt it had a sexier ring to it. Other titles considered at this time were 'Zinc Rider', 'Sonic Bones', 'Tank' and 'Pretty Shepherdess'.

He also juggled with the track listing for some time, even proposing to include 'Sunken Rags', 'Truck On (Tyke)', 'Mighty Shepherdess', 'Sudden Alley Boogie' and 'Shadowhead', but decided to shelve these songs for possible future release.

An untampered acoustic version of the title track can be found on the 'Rarities One' album (a 1990 fan club release)

Highest chart position: No. 4

TANX
Released: 23rd March, 1973 (EMI-T.Rex Wax Co.)
Producer: Tony Visconti

The original proof for the 'Tanx' album had to be withdrawn, as it was thought to be too provocative.

This was the second of the albums to include a free poster (the poster inside was also a shot from the 'Tanx' sessions) and the first official follow-up album release not to include song lyrics.

Untampered acoustic versions of 'Tenement Lady' and other tracks from 'Tanx' can be found on the 'Rarities One' album (*ibid*).

Highest chart position: No. 4

GREAT HITS
Released: 19th October, 1973 (EMI-T.Rex Wax Co.)
Producer: Tony Visconti

This was the last album to include a free poster (a colour shot of Marc in concert).

Although entitled 'Great Hits', 'The Slider' and 'Shock Rock' were both album tracks from respectively, 'The Slider' and 'Tanx'.

It is worth noting that, although '20th Century Boy' has always been credited to

Visconti as producer, Mick O'Halloran insists that Marc produced this track, in the absence of Visconti.

This was the last 'Hits' album released in Marc's lifetime.

Highest chart position: No. 32

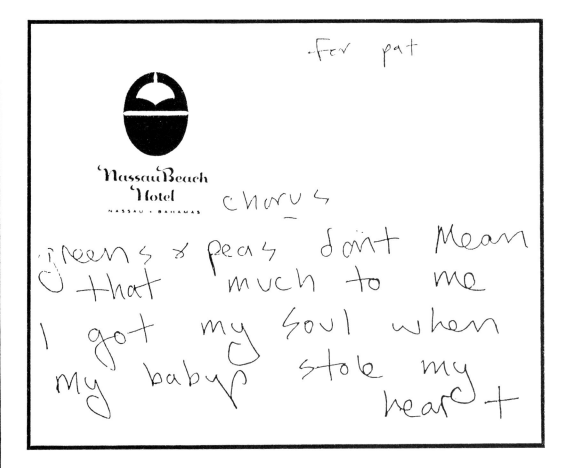

Marc's personal notes for the never-released Pat Hall LP (Pat was one of Marc's backing vocalists from 1973-4, and was originally recommended to him by Gloria Jones). Although the album was completed and mixed by Marc, the tapes were shelved indefinitely. Tracks would have included 'Do Your Thing', 'Jitterbug Love', 'City Port' and 'When I Was A Child'.

ZINC ALLOY AND THE HIDDEN RIDERS OF TOMORROW OR A CREAMED CAGE IN AUGUST
Released: 1st February, 1974 (EMI-T.Rex Wax Co.)
Producer: Tony Visconti/Marc Bolan

The 'Zinc' album was the only LP credited, in Marc's lifetime, to 'Marc Bolan and T.Rex'.

The album was also available as a limited edition of ten thousand copies in a special multi-fold cut-out sleeve. These were only available through competitions in the media, although a small quantity did find their way into some shops.

Various tracks were retitled, added and omitted from the album, as follows: 'Painless Persuasion' was originally entitled 'Look To Your Soul'. Originally included were 'Sitting Here', 'Truck On (Tyke)', 'Dance In The Midnight' and 'Saturday Night', but these were replaced by 'Sound Pit', 'Explosive Mouth' and 'Teenage Dream'. Other tracks were also recorded at the Munich sessions, including 'Hope You Enjoy The Show' (a kind of slowed down version of 'Satisfaction Pony') and the very bluesy 'Plateau Skull'. Both of these can be found on the 'Rarities Three' album (*ibid*).

Untampered/incomplete mixes and alternative versions from the 'Zinc Alloy' sessions can be heard on the 'Rarities Two' LP (*ibid*).

Highest chart position: No. 12

THE BEGINNING OF DOVES
Released: 22nd June, 1974 (Track Records)
Producer: Simon Napier-Bell

In 1972, Marc obtained an injunction to prevent the release of early demos called 'Hard On Love'. Two years later, the album surfaced under the new title, 'The Beginning Of Doves'. Marc was unhappy with the release, as he felt that it was unrepresentative of where, at the time, he was at.

Highest chart position: Non-entry

BOLAN'S ZIP-GUN
Released: 11th March, 1977 (EMI-T.Rex Wax Co.)
Producer: Marc Bolan

This was the second official follow-up that did not include printed song lyrics and the only album cover that did not mention T.Rex on the sleeve; Marc's début album as solo producer, it was the last LP to feature Mickey Finn. 'Zip-Gun' was also one of only two albums to feature a cut-out sleeve design.

An untampered version (rough take) of 'Solid Baby' can be found on 'Rarities Three' (*ibid*).

Highest chart position: Non-entry

FUTURISTIC DRAGON
Released: 31st January, 1976 (EMI-T.Rex Wax Co.)
Producer: Marc Bolan

This album featured the so-called 'comeback' singles, 'New York City' and 'Dreamy Lady'. An alternative/rough take of 'All Alone' can be found on the 'Rarities Two' album (*ibid*), under Marc's tentative title of 'Saturation Syncopation'.

Highest chart position: No. 50

Marc signing an autograph for a young fan outside the Granada Studios in Manchester after filming one of the *Marc* shows, Aug/Sept, 1977.

DANDY IN THE UNDERWORLD
Released: 11th March, 1977 (EMI-T.Rex Wax Co.)
Producer: Marc Bolan

Originally called 'Teen Riot Structure', the 'Dandy' LP was Marc's last album released before he died. The sleeve was the second to feature a cut-out design and had dedications on the inner jacket to Rolan (Marc and Gloria's son), Beau (Harry Nilsson's son) and Felix and Parker (the sons of Marc's manager, Tony Howard).

The album featured the track 'Visions Of Domino', a song that Marc had originally written and performed as 'Funky London Childhood' in 1975, and he had planned to use it in a concept project known as the 'London Opera' (which would also have included 'London Boys'). Marc eventually rewrote the words, kept the backing track and changed the title to 'Visions of Domino'.

It also appears that 'To Know Him Is To Love Him' was considered for inclusion, but was eventually deemed out of context in relation to the rest of the album.

Highest chart position: No. 26

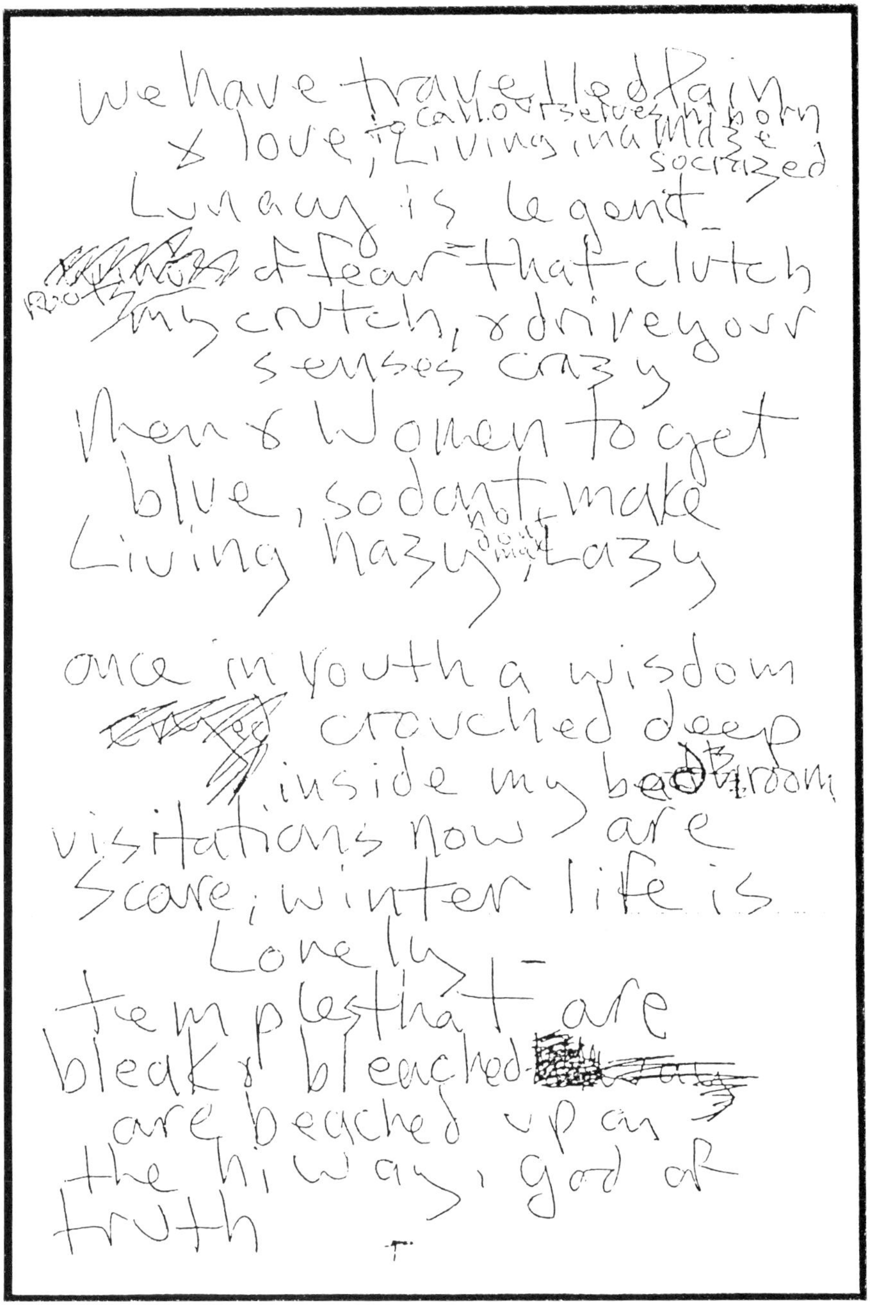

We have travelled Pain
& love, Living in a maze
to call ourselves ... born
socialized
Lunacy is le gout
... of fear that clutch
my crutch, & drive your
senses crazy
Men & Women to get
blue, so dont make
Living hazy ... Lazy

once in youth a wisdom
crouched deep
inside my bedroom
visitations now are
scare, winter life is
Lonely —
temples that are
bleak & bleached
are beached up on
the hiway, god of
truth

Left: Marc's handwritten notes for the 'Dandy' LP.

Above: Handwritten 'Pain and Love' lyrics, Marc's eerie offering to the 'Dandy' album, 1977.

1 →Jason b sade   1 Dandy
2 Crimson moon   2 groove a little
3 universe   3 Suit
4 Im a fool for you 4 hang ups
5 ~~xxxxxx~~ I love to boog 5 Pain x love
6 visions of Domino 6 teen riot structu

5 · secs   (final)

1 Dandy   1 →Jason b sade
2 Crimson Moon   2 groove a little
3 univeRse   3 Suit
4 fool for you   4 hang ups
5 I Love to boogie   5 Pain x Love
6 visions of domino 6 teen riot structu

single
groove a little
Suit
→ Jason

teen riot structure ancle deep in fear
baby lost in bellies & the people cant
hear a demon angel demigod
blasted thru the night & me
& lucy lightning holding on real
tight.

a tempest teen of stature in gatsby
hat & cloak licked upon
my lolipop but I couldn't get
the joke

all London was in ashes burning to
the sound of deep galactic
tragedy in a seraphim
sound

its a teen riot structure
just a teen riot structure

Left: Marc's track listing for the 'Dandy in the Underworld' LP, and notes for single releases.

Above: Handwritten lyrics to 'Teen Riot Structure' from the 'Dandy' LP. The line 'licked upon my lollipop. . .' referred to the 'joke-on-a-stick' iced lollies popular in the '70s.

teen riot structure
Low synth chords down
synth strings on end.

Solo hi aranged fuzz
        hendrix tone
- Piana acustic slowed
down on, F to G bit
                    Riff
tracked
tamberine double time on CAFG
                voices
straight punk till, repeat of
first verse then, 1st tracked
+ low tracked in unison
on CAFG, m3y hi very speed
+ maz, lowed down,
        its justa teen riot
        amps then waw
                        waw

Left: Marc's chord sequences and arrangements for 'Teen Riot Structure'.

Above: Handwritten lyrics to 'Messing with the Mystic', a rough draft of a song that might have been included on the follow-up album to 'Dandy in the Underworld'.

```
        YOUNG GIRL OF LOVE.


        young girl of love where are you now
        young girl of love.


    I, shoulder pads & scottish plaids could always turn me on
        synphones like stormy seas, & cocktails that are strong


    "2. fotographs in sepia & paintings that are old,

        seeing you in lectric blue & sunsets that are gold


    3,. fantasies of modern art, make motion like a train
        locomotive disco beat to drive this boy in sane.
```

? verses, then organ
3rd verse then long fade on hook — 8 times

    —two saxes -da- da- dada— x ooo h bit
    —string section ·   ↗ gloria - d tracked
    —percussinist
    —electric - big chords - 4 tracked
    —4 acurstics mix to one, real tight.

            {——————————————————————{

Lyrics and handwritten arrangements for 'Young Girl of Love', another song that in finished form might have gone onto the follow-up album to 'Dandy in the Underworld'.

Marc inside his vintage white Rolls Royce on his way to EMI Records for a photo session to promote the forthcoming 'Solid Gold' album in September, 1977. Marc had personally selected all the tracks for this 'Greatest Hits' LP but, sadly, it was not released until 8th June, 1979, nearly two years after his death.

do I love thee

have you seen her
funky girl, like a
cat in a storm

We have loved
her since the
day that the
earth was
born

music matter as
the blind who
hear eyes that
see

do I love thee do I
love thee yea

Marc's original handwritten lyrics to 'Do I Love Thee'. This song was released after Marc's death, on the 1983 album 'Dance in the Midnight'.

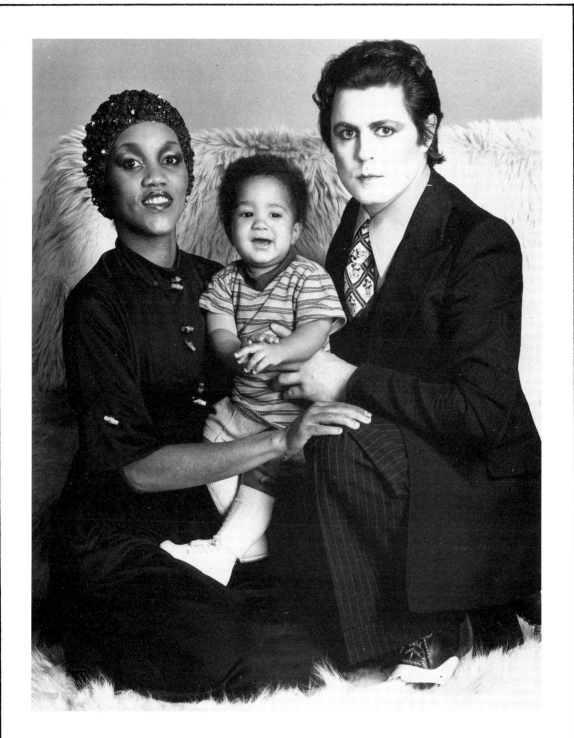

'It's a shame for man to hide all the things that do survive from his past. . .'

SOURCES AND ACKNOWLEDGEMENTS

The photographers (where known) are Mary Bullen, pages 26 (top and bottom) and 113; Steev Burgess, p.30; Harry Goodwin, pp.86 and 98; Granada TV, p103; Steven Gridley, p.81 (top); Christine Isherwood, p.99; Margaret Nolan, pp.105 and 165; Tony Prime, pp.2, 39, 40-41 and 43; David Rooney, pp.106 (top and bottom) and 173; Nikki Sudden, pp.73, 78 and 96 (top and bottom); Caron Thomas, pp.6, 81 (bottom), 114, 115, 116, 117, 118, 120, 124, 125, 126, 127, 130 and 131 (bottom). All the photographs are from the collection of John Willans and Caron Thomas with the exceptions of those made available by Boz Boorer, p.47; Ros Davies, p.63; and EMI, p.145. All photographs are copyright © the photographers and licensers detailed above.

The prose and poems printed on pages 60, 62, 62-5, 67, 68 and 69, and the manuscripts and drawings reproduced on pages 61, 68, 71, 72, 74, 75, 76, 77, 79, 80, 82, 83, 84, 85, 90, 92, 93, 100, 104, 128, 133, 137, 141, 142, 149, 150, 151, 153, 159, 160, 161, 163, 166, 167, 168, 169, 170, 171, 172 and 174 are copyright © the Estate of Marc Bolan. All are from the collection of John Willans and Caron Thomas, with the exceptions of those made available by Ros Davies, pp.79, 100, 104, 149, 150 and 171; Keith Harrop, pp.60, 61 and 62-5; Uwe Klee, pp.14 and 15; George Rab, pp.141 and 142; and the T. Rex Offices, pp.21, 153, 160, 161 and 172. The items on pages 69, 71, 80, 128, 151, 166 and 167 were given by Marc Bolan to Caron Thomas, and those on pages 79, 100, 104, 149, 150 and 171 to Ros Davies. The items on pages 85, 90, 92, 93, 133, 137, 159, 168, 169, 170 and 174 were given by Mr and Mrs Feld to John Willans and Caron Thomas. Most of the remaining items were acquired from dealers or at auction.

The line 'I need TV when I got T. Rex' quoted on page 87 is from 'All The Young Dudes' by David Bowie, copyright © 1971 by Bewlay Brothers Music/Fleur Music, USA, reproduced by permission of EMI Music Publishing Ltd, London WC2H 0EA, and Chrysalis Music Ltd. The lines from 'Rip It Up' by John Marascalo and Robert Blackwell are copyright © 1956 by Venice Music Inc., USA, reproduced by permission of Peter Maurice Music Co. Ltd, London WC2H 0EA. The lyrics of 'Ride A White Swan' (page 137) and the words 'Fleetfoot Voodoo Man' quoted on page 33 from 'Rip Off', both written by Marc Bolan, are copyright © 1970 by Westminster Music Ltd, all rights reserved, used by permission. The lyrics of 'Laser Love' (page 149), 'Life's an Elevator' (page 150), 'City Port' (page 151), 'Pain and Love' (page 167), 'Teen Riot Structure' (page 169) and 'Do I Love Thee' (page 174), together with the line 'In sheer dazzling raiment' (page 107) from 'Futuristic Dragon', all by Marc Bolan, are copyright © Wizard (Bahamas) Ltd, reprinted by permission of Wizard (Bahamas) Ltd.

Every effort has been made to locate photographers and copyright-holders, but in the event of any omissions the publishers would be grateful to hear from any such parties so that they can be rectified in future editions of the book.